Re-Reading Margery Kempe in the 21st Century

Erratum

Misprinted ISBN on the back cover.
Correct ISBN:
978-3-0343-0642-3

Valentina Castagna

Re-Reading Margery Kempe in the 21st Century

PETER LANG
Bern · Berlin · Bruxelles · Frankfurt am Main · New York · Oxford · Wien

Bibliographic information published by Die Deutsche Nationalbibliothek
Die Deutsche Nationalbibliothek lists this publication in the Deutsche National-
bibliografie; detailed bibliographic data is available on the Internet at
‹http://dnb.d-nb.de›.

British Library and Library of Congress Cataloguing-in-Publication Data:
A catalogue record for this book is available from *The British Library*,
Great Britain.

Library of Congress Cataloging-in-Publication Data

Castagna, Valentina.
Re-reading Margery Kempe in the 21st century / Valentina Castagna.
p. cm.
Includes bibliographical references.
ISBN 978-3-0343-0642-3
1. Kempe, Margery, b. ca. 1373. Book of Margery Kempe. 2. Christian literature, English (Middle)–History and criticism. 3. Authors, English–Middle English, 1100-1500–Biography. 4. Christian women–Religious life–England–History–To 1500. 5. Dissenters, Religious–England–History–To 1500. 6. Mysticism–England–History–Middle Ages, 600-1500. I. Title.
PR2007.K4Z63 2011
248.2'2092–dc22
[B]
                                2011006644

Cover design: Thomas Jaberg, Peter Lang AG

ISBN 978-3-0343-0642-3

© Peter Lang AG, International Academic Publishers, Bern 2011
Hochfeldstrasse 32, CH-3012 Bern, Switzerland
info@peterlang.com, www.peterlang.com, www.peterlang.net

All rights reserved.
All parts of this publication are protected by copyright.
Any utilisation outside the strict limits of the copyright law, without the
permission of the publisher, is forbidden and liable to prosecution.
This applies in particular to reproductions, translations, microfilming, and
storage and processing in electronic retrieval systems.

Printed in Switzerland

For my mother

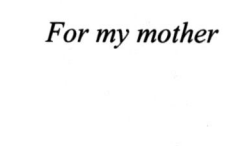

Acknowledgements

My extreme gratitude goes to Prof. Daniela Corona for her guidance and support and Prof. Elio Di Piazza for his suggestions and encouragement. I am indebted to Anthony Bale, my supervisor at Birkbeck College in 2005, who directed my attention towards challenging new approaches to *The Book of Margery Kempe*.

Table of Contents

INTRODUCTION
New Perspectives on *The Book of Margery Kempe* 11
    Critical approaches: past and present 13
    Literary authority and literary genres 17
    Sexuality, gender and performance 20

CHAPTER 1
Autobiography and Mystic Text 25
    Complexity and modernity 27
    Strategies of legitimization 33

CHAPTER 2
Travels of/on Her Own 43
    From Lynn to the Holy Land via Italy 48

CHAPTER 3
Abjection and the Body 59
    Gender and *queer* performances 62
    Subverting the process of abjection 69

CHAPTER 4
A Contemporary Re-Writing:
Eva Figes's *The True Tale of Margery Kempe* 77
    Back to orality 78
    Sexuality and virginity 81

Conclusions 85
References 91

INTRODUCTION

New Perspectives on
The Book of Margery Kempe[1]

This book takes into consideration more radical interpretations and rewritings of *The Book of Margery Kempe* from various contemporary critical perspectives and from a creative point of view. This work offers a particular focus on gender and sexuality in the representation of the public roles assumed by Margery Kempe as a mystic, (outlaw) preacher and pilgrim. Over the last decade of the 20th century and the first decade of the 21st century, Margery Kempe's text and character have received increasing critical attention, and more than other contemporary mystics and their texts, from scholars interested not only in the field of Medieval Studies but also the fields of Women Studies, Gender Studies and more recently Queer Studies. At the same time, Margery and her *Book* have become a powerful source of inspiration for unconventional authors interested in the interconnections of spirituality and sexuality and in her *queerness*.

We shall be taking into examination the way in which the representation of Margery in her public roles is analyzed more and more frequently in terms of gender and by making reference to the concepts of performance and *queerness*. We shall also be drawing attention to some of the issues emerging from the widely-accepted definition of the book as the first autobiography in English, as re-

---

1   The first version of this chapter was presented as a paper at the 24th AIA Conference "Challenges for the 21st Century: Dilemmas, Ambiguities, Directions", University of Roma 3 (Italy), literature workshop, and was accepted for publication in the conference proceedings (forthcoming).

gards the concept of authorship, and consequently to the role of Margery Kempe as "author"[2]. This is a view that, as we shall see, has come to be widely shared by many contemporary scholars and not only those militating within Women's Studies. As one of the most prolific critics to contribute to fresh perspectives on *The Book of Margery Kempe* in the 1990s, Lynn Staley Johnson affirms that her work on this book has convinced her that "studies of Kempe's artistry are well justified but that we need to apply to Kempe the complicated series of questions about narrative that we apply to other major authors of the medieval period"[3].

As Sidonie Smith and Julia Watson maintain, readers should be aware of the original cultural and historical contexts because, "when a medieval mystic such as Margery Kempe dictated her narrative to an amanuensis, she didn't understand herself as an "author" with ownership rights in her story",[4] a statement which draws attention to the role of the relationship between author and scribe. Susan Morrison, working on the representation of women pilgrims in late medieval England, also puts the spotlight on Margery as author of her book, highlighting Kempe's use of the most common *topoi* of

---

[2] In contemporary re-readings, both the vernacular text and its translations into modern English have been the object of analyses focusing on the recovery of Margery's voice as authorial voice, not only in the field of Women's Studies but also in the field of Autobiography/Life Writing Studies. These works focus both on the study of the literary genre and the questions related to the presence of the scribes and on the question of agency. In this book, the quotations from the text are from Sanford Brown Meech and Hope Emily Allen's edition (London: Oxford University Press, 1940) and are followed by Barry Windeatt's translation (Harmondsworth: Penguin, 1985) – henceforth abbreviated as Meech and Allen and Windeatt.

[3] L. Staley Johnson, *Margery Kempe's Dissenting Fiction* (University Park, Pennsylvania: The Pennsylvania State University Press, 1994), p. 2.

[4] S. Smith and J. Watson, *Reading Autobiography. A Guide for Interpreting Life Narratives* (second edition, Minneapolis: University of Minnesota Press, 2010), p. 237.

women pilgrims of the time – erotic, sacred, threatening – thus showing she is "deliberately crafting her work"[5].

Critical approaches: past and present

The history of *The Book of Margery Kempe* – dictated by a burgess of Bishop's Lynn (now King's Lynn, Norfolk) between 1436 and 1438 –, is quite revealing of the way Medieval Studies have entered the 21st century. Its links with the present have become stronger thanks to the critical approach, initially of Women's Studies and then of Gender Studies[6], to the issues of authorship, sexuality and the body, and ultimately of *performance*[7].

---

5   S. S. Morrison, *Women Pilgrims in Late Medieval England. Private Piety as Public Performance* (New York: Routledge, 2000), p. 128.
6   See N. F. Partner "Studying Medieval Women. Sex, Gender, Feminism", *Speculum*, 68, 2 (1993), pp. 305-308; and also J. Bennett, "Medievalism and Feminism", in Partner N. F. (ed.), *Studying Medieval Women. Sex, Gender, Feminism* (Cambridge, Massachussetts: The Medieval Academy of America, 1993), pp. 7-29. We shall also be seeing how some representatives of Queer Studies have contributed to giving new life to Margery Kempe's text. This is the case with Carolyn Dinshaw with her essay "Margery Kempe Writes Back" included in her study *Getting Medieval: Sexualities and Communities, Pre- and Postmodern* (Durham: Duke University Press, 1999), pp. 143-182, in the critical field, and of Robert Glück, with his novel *Margery Kempe* (London: Serpent's Tail, 1994), in the creative field.
7   See L. McAvoy, "Virgin, Mother, Whore: The Sexual Spirituality of Margery Kempe", in Chewning S. M. (ed.), *Intersections of Sexuality and the Divine in Medieval Culture: The Word Made Flesh* (Aldershot: Ashgate, 2005), pp. 121-138; C. Bradford, "Mother, Maiden, Child: Gender as Performance in *The Book of Margery Kempe*", in Devlin-Glass F. and L. McCredden (eds), *Feminist Poetics of the Sacred: Creative Suspicions* (Oxford: Oxford University Press, 2001), pp. 165-181; and N. Hopenwasser, "A Performance Artist and Her Performance Text: Margery Kempe on

13

As Lynn Staley Johnson pointed out at the end of the last century, the revision of the literary canon has "allowed texts like *The Book of Margery Kempe* into the classroom, the conference hall and the journal"[8]. Staley Johnson added that, although the appreciation of Kempe's work had drastically increased in the '80s and '90s, *The Book of Margery Kempe* "ha[d] more still to teach us"[9]. Actually, since then, criticism has investigated themes which had formerly been overlooked; many scholars have quite recently been working on the representation of sexuality, on the relationship between spirituality and fasting, and on her travel accounts as a pilgrim[10].

In the 15th and 16th centuries, the book had acquired quite a wide readership, especially in monasteries (where it must have been read by both monks and laywomen)[11]. However, after the Anglican schism, the text was lost for five centuries. The manuscript was surprisingly rediscovered by William Butler-Bowdon in 1934 and subsequently published by Meech and Allen.

Until that time, the name of Margery Kempe had been well-known through the excerpts from her book, which Wynkyn de Worde and, later, Henry Pepwell had copied out at the beginning of the 16th century. These were the most canonical passages in the

---

Tour", in Suydam M. A. and J. E. Ziegler (eds), *Performance and Transformation: New Approaches to Late Medieval Spirituality* (New York: St. Martin's Press, 1999), pp. 97-131.

8   L. Staley Johnson, *Margery Kempe's Dissenting Fictions*, p. xi.

9   *Ibidem*.

10 On fasting see G. Del Lungo Camiciotti, "Il significato del digiuno nell'esperienza delle mistiche inglesi tardo medievali", *LC. Rivista Online del Dipartimento di Letterature e Culture Europee* II, 1 (2008), pp. 63-75, <http://www.dilce.unipa.it/rivista/documenti/n_01_2008/09_g_dellungo.pdf> last accessed December 2009; on Margery's pilgrimages see A. Goodman, *Margery Kempe and Her World* (London & New York: Longman, 2002).

11 See K. Parsons, "The Red Ink Annotator of *The Book of Margery Kempe* and his Lay Audience", in Kerby-Fulton K. and M. Hilmo (eds), *The Medieval Professional Reader at Work: Evidence from Manuscripts of Chaucer, Langland, Kempe and Gower* (Victoria: ELS University of Victoria, 2001), pp. 143-158.

book and they only stressed one aspect of Margery's personality: her devoutness. Such readings were mostly misleading, with Pepwell, for instance, adding to his text that the extracts were from the life of a devout anchoress, which Margery was not. The complexity and modernity of *The Book of Margery Kempe* were totally disregarded. It is interesting to see how George Ballard described *The Book* and its authoress in the 18th century in his volume *Memoirs of Several Ladies of Great Britain: Who Have Been Celebrated for Their Writings or Skill in the Learned Languages, Arts, and Sciences* (1752), in which he included an entry on Margery Kempe:

> [Margery Kempe] and her writings are so little known to the learned world, that she has escaped the knowledge even of the indefatigable compiler of the Typographical antiquities, who seems an intire [sic] stranger to her book, which is now become so extremely scarce, that I can hear of no more than two copies extant [...] [12].

In his comments on the disappearance of the original text (he was able to trace two copies of de Worde's version), and considering how little he knew of her life, the figure of Margery, nonetheless, definitely emerges as one of an "author"[13].

It is therefore thanks to scholars working within the field of Gender studies right since the 1990s, that the book has raised more complex and challenging issues and is now being read, in Sidonie Smith's terms, as

> a fascinating work, full of life and energy and travail as it captures the quality of medieval Christian life, the mobile atmosphere of pilgrimages, the

---

12   G. Ballard, "Memoirs of Margery Kempe", in *Memoirs of Several Ladies of Great Britain: Who Have Been Celebrated for Their Writings or Skill in the Learned Languages, Arts, and Sciences* (Oxford: printed by W. Jackson for the author, 1752), p. 8.
13   *Ibidem*.

pressures of orthodoxy, the smell of the burning stake against which the heretic was pressed in her heresy.[14]

The first readings of the book focused on the figure of Margery either as a mystic or as a hysteric, if not both[15]. Her mystical experience was a target for criticism and was seen as non-canonical. As Lynn Staley Johnson, one of her major contemporary critics, has stated, those distinguished scholars were mostly interested in the history of mysticism and in devotional prose[16]. The traditional comparison with her contemporary anchoress Julian of Norwich, viewed as a canonical mystic-theologian, was based on stereotypes of gender. Whereas Julian was the epitome of placidity, Margery was deemed to be a hysteric, a rather peculiar mystic. However, because of its constant references to Margery's experience as a pilgrim, an "outlaw preacher", a woman and a wife (especially, her relationship with her husband, her pilgrimages, and money matters), her eccentric text of mystical writing has now found its place within the canon of English literature as an *ante-litteram* autobiography. In fact, *The Book of Margery Kempe* is now widely recognized as the first autobiography in English[17].

14 S. Smith, "The Book of Margery Kempe: This Creature's Unsealed Life", in *A Poetics of Women's Autobiography* (Bloomington: Indiana University Press, 1987), p. 60.
15 H. Thurston, "Margery the Astonishing", *The Month* 168 (1936), pp. 446-456; K. Cholmeley, *Margery Kempe. Genius and Mystic* (London: Green & Co., 1947); E. I. Watkin, "In Defence of Margery Kempe", in *Poets and Mystics* (London: Sheed and Ward, 1953), pp. 104-134; D. Knowles, *The English Mystical Tradition* (London: Burns and Oates, 1961); G. Wood Tuma, *The Fourteenth Century English Mystics: A Comparative Analysis* (Salzburg: Universitat Salzburg, 1977).
16 Lynn Staley Johnson, *Margery Kempe's Dissenting Fictions*, p. xi.
17 See J. M. Mueller, "Autobiography of a New 'Creatur': Female Spirituality, Selfhood, and Authorship in *The Book of Margery Kempe*", in Stanton D. (ed.), *The Female Autograph* (Chicago: The University of Chicago Press, 1984), pp. 57-68; S. Smith, "The Book of Margery Kempe: This Creature's Unsealed Life"; C. Glenn, "Author, Audience, and Autobiography: Rhetori-

Literary authority and literary genres

The Book, then, has been defined as an autobiography, as a spiritual autobiography of a laywoman, a devotional treatise (the "Proem" itself defines the book as such), an oral life-story, and also the first novel in English[18]. The problem of placing it in a particular literary genre arises, on the one hand, from the textual presence of the scribes and, on the other, from the content of Margery's narrative. Her account abounds in details from daily life and material preoccupation, which must have led the first modern readers to think that Margery's mysticism was not genuine, perhaps too materialistic, particularly when compared to Julian of Norwich, whose works are more orthodox.

The complexity of this medieval text (and of its female authorial voice) is acknowledged and throws up issues that are still hotly debated in contemporary literature, such as women's identity, female authorship, and the influence of patriarchal society on the relaying of women's image. David Aers maintained that *The Book of Margery Kempe* is "a precious work for anyone interested in the history of gender, subjectivities, and English culture"[19].

---

cal Technique in *The Book of Margery Kempe*", *College English* 54, 5 (1992), pp. 540-553; see also the *Dictionary of Literary Terms & Literary Theory*, ed. by J. A. Cuddon (London: Penguin, 1999). On Autobiography Studies, in Italy, see Chialant M. T. and Bottalico M. (eds), *L'impulso autobiografico* (Napoli: Liguori, 2005) and, in particular on women's autobiography, see Carla Locatelli's essay, "Is S/(he) My Gaze? (Feminist) Possibilities for Autobiographical Co(n)texts", within the same book, pp. 3-18.

[18] See respectively, G. Del Lungo Camiciotti (ed.), *Il libro di Margery Kempe. Autobiografia spirituale di una laica del Quattrocento* (Milano: Àncora, 2002); R. C. Ross, "Oral Life, Written Text: The Genesis of *The Book of Margery Kempe*", *The Yearbook of English Studies* 22 (1992), pp. 226-237; and L. Staley Johnson, *Margery Kempe's Dissenting Fictions*.

[19] D. Aers, *Community, Gender and Individual Identity. English Writing 1360-1430* (London: Routledge, 1988), p. 73.

Scholars such as Smith, Staley Johnson and Mueller have quite recently come to show that Margery, as we shall be seeing, establishes her literary authority through the use of clear narrative strategies. Although the intervention of the scribes to whom she dictates her experience, is to a certain degree undeniable[20], it emerges from events, especially from Margery's comments on gender roles and her arguments with religious and political authorities, that Margery is aware of the idea of authority, which she sees, above all, in the external Authority of God (i.e. that which legitimates her text, travels, and public-speaking)[21].

The positions of such scholars and their focus on the concept of authorship have as their basis the idea that Margery is not the illiterate creature she claims to be, but an author following the narrative conventions of literary genres like the Lives of the Saints and those used by other women mystics who had recorded their experiences before her. Besides, as Mulder-Bakker and McAvoy point out, it is crucial to rethink the relationship between women and learning, and women's knowledge of the Holy Scripture and religious texts in general. They maintain that terms like "illiterate" should be contextualized within a society, medieval society, in

---

[20] Lynn Staley Johnson maintains that the figure of the scribe might be a trope, one of Margery's strategies to legitimize her role as author, since the use of scribes was common. She goes as far as to define Margery's book as a "novel". See L. Staley Johnson, "The Trope of the Scribe and the Question of Literary Authority in the Works of Julian of Norwich and Margery Kempe", *Speculum*, LXVI (1991), pp. 820-838. Carolyn Dinshaw, on her part, responds to Staley Johnson's hypothesis by affirming that, though quite stimulating, her view would not explain some gaps in the narrative "that suggest the priest never stopped worrying about what he suspected to be Margery's excessive devotional manner". See C. Dinshaw, "Margery Kempe Writes Back", p. 159.

[21] On the relationship between authority and agency see S. Beckwith, "Problems of Authority in Late Medieval English Mysticism: Language, Agency, and Authority in *The Book of Margery Kempe*", *Exemplaria*, 4, 1 (1992), pp. 171-199.

which "public orality" and "community of discourse" were prominent means of learning[22].

Margery also shows that she is aware of the social conventions that might silence her, but is able to make use of them – mining the system of oppression from within – by legitimizing herself through her mystical relationship with Christ.

Thus, in the analysis of medieval texts, the gendered approach has acquired ever greater importance, also through its attempt to rediscover a genealogy of women writers[23]. Smith, in particular, considers Margery as a forerunner of women's autobiographical writing[24].

In the 1990s it became clear that the main instrument for interpreting Kempe's narrative was the laying bare of those social mechanisms that determined the subaltern role of women within the family and society. This reading has empowered Kempe as an authoress and at the same time has highlighted Kempe's strategies of self-empowerment, not only in the private but also in the public domain.

Most recent readings show that Margery actually understood the role of the mystics' writings among both religious and lay people, and

---

[22] A. B. Mulder-Bakker and L. McAvoy, "Experientia and the Construction of Experience in Medieval Writing: An Introduction", in Mulder-Bakker A. B. and L. McAvoy (eds), *Women and Experience in Later Medieval Writing: Reading the Book of Life* (New York: Palgrave Macmillan, 2009), p. 9. On Margery Kempe's illiteracy see also Tarvers J. K., "The Alleged Illiteracy of Margery Kempe: A Reconsideration of the Evidence", *Medieval Perspectives*, 11 (1996), pp. 113-124.

[23] See S. Smith, "The Book of Margery Kempe: This Creature's Unsealed Life" and J. M. Mueller, "Autobiography of a New 'Creatur': Female Spirituality, Selfhood, and Authorship in *The Book of Margery Kempe*".

[24] S. Smith, "The Book of Margery Kempe: This Creature's Unsealed Life", p. 42. See also Glenn C., "Reexamining *The Book of Margery Kempe*: A Rhetoric of Autobiography", in Lunsford A. (ed.), *Reclaiming Rhetorica: Women in the Rhetorical Tradition* (Pittsburgh: University of Pittsburgh Press, 1995), pp. 53-71.

made good use of them in legitimizing her own act of writing and the inherent attempt, through the text, to claim her own subjectivity.

Sexuality, gender and performance

As mentioned above, a second question which has aroused the interest of Margery Kempe's critics is the interplay of spirituality and sexuality in the text, the way in which Margery tells of her private "dalliance" with Christ. Her language shows the main characteristics of "mystic speech" and she demonstrates her knowledge of mystic texts by both mentioning them and in the way she describes her divine communication with God, this being like a fire burning her from the inside. The term "dalyawnce" itself implies a form of 'sexual' intimacy in the conversation. Windeatt maintains that Margery Kempe had "evidently been affected" by Richard Rolle's work and later comments on Rolle's *Incendium Amoris* and the use of bodily language, saying that its "sensory qualities could encourage the impressionable to mistake merely physical sensations for mystical experience"[25].

25 B. Windeatt, "Introductory Essay" to *English Mystics of the Middle Ages* (Cambridge: Cambridge University Press, 1994), pp. 2-3. Caroline Walker Bynum has argued that the availability of the vernacular languages profoundly influenced women's writing in the Middle Ages because, unlike Latin, the vernacular allowed them to use an experiential style and language which characterized the most popular literary genres of the time, love poetry and romantic stories. This, according to Bynum, led to the use of language based on the senses and on physicality. See C. Walker Bynum, "The Female Body and Religious Practice in the Later Middle Ages", in *Fragmentation and Redemption. Essays on Gender and the Human Body in Medieval Religion* (New York: Zone Books, 1991), p. 196. On Margery Kempe's mystical language and its materialism, see Beckwith S , "A Very Material Mysticism: The Medieval Mysticism of Margery Kempe", in Aers

This is an issue that has triggered different responses at both a critical and a creative level, in terms of rewriting. Eva Figes's dramatization of the Book in *The True Tale of Margery Kempe*, for instance, simply modifies the text by including in its dialogues "sounds of love-making"[26]. In the title of her radio play, the writer stresses, at the same time, the strong relationship between orality and writing and the link to popular culture. By doing so she emphasises Margery's preoccupation with desire and pleasure, which, as we shall see, are a hindrance to her holiness, and in direct contrast to her enactment of chastity through her adoption of the white robe and the ring.

Another interesting work of fiction inspired by *The Book of Margery Kempe* is the provocative 1994 novel by Robert Glück entitled *Margery Kempe*[27], which supports the idea of Margery's *queerness* (also analysed in Carolyn Dinshaw's 1999 study *Getting Medieval*)[28]. Glück specifically draws inspiration from Margery's sexual drives and creates a double narrative rich in physical detail, where he interweaves her love for the young Christ, narrated at the beginning of the *Book*, with his love for a young man[29].

All these responses together render the debate on *The Book of Margery Kempe* more lively and highlight the physicality of Margery's language, not only when in mystical conversation with Christ, but also when confronting her adversaries.

D. (ed.), *Medieval Literature. Criticism, Ideology and History* (Brighton: Harvester Press, 1986), pp. 34-57.
26 E. Figes, *The True Tale of Margery Kempe* (London: BBC Radio 2, 1985).
27 R. Glück, *Margery Kempe*.
28 C. Dinshaw, "Margery Kempe Writes Back".
29 Another work of certain interest, which however mixes creative writing and historical research, is L. Collis's *Memoirs of a Medieval Woman: The Life and Times of Margery Kempe* (New York: Thomas Y. Crowell Company, 1964).

In her interesting article "Virgin, Mother, Whore: The Sexual Spirituality of Margery Kempe"[30], published a mere few years ago, Liz McAvoy argues that Judith Butler's critique of the notion of fixed gender identities and her theory of performative gender are suited to an analysis of the way Margery Kempe portrays herself. In fact, Butler suggests that gender is constituted by a series of performed acts, "gestures, enactments, generally construed" which are

> performative in the sense that the essence or identity that they otherwise purport to express are fabrications manufactured and sustained through corporeal signs and other discursive means[31].

Drawing on Butler's positions, McAvoy argues that Margery, like other medieval women, was "able to negotiate with [her] sexualized bod[y] the restrictive hegemony of gendered identity"[32]. McAvoy demonstrates how, through the "re-appropriation" of the roles of the virgin, or of the mother, Margery might attain a social position from which to speak and express herself, thus recovering "agency in her re/construction of self with which much of her text is occupied"[33].

McAvoy, in fact, maintains that if

> Margery's gendered body as wife or mother has no specific ontology beyond the acts which help to constitute its 'reality', then contained within these acts is always the potential for re-contextualisation and therefore subversion of their traditional hegemony[34].

In other words, Kempe re-appropriates these social roles, playing with gender stereotypes based on female sexuality, and enacts

30 L. McAvoy, "Virgin, Mother, Whore: The Sexual Spirituality of Margery Kempe".
31 J. Butler, *Gender Trouble* (London: Routledge, 1990), p. 136.
32 L. McAvoy, "Virgin, Mother, Whore: The Sexual Spirituality of Margery Kempe", p. 122.
33 *Ibidem.*
34 *Ibid.*, p. 124.

them in order to be legitimized by the system (which denies women's agency) as an independent woman, speaking up for herself. It is well known that, whereas, on the one hand, medieval women's bodies were important for their bestowing of a reproductive capacity, on the other, they were feared and demonized because they were considered a corrupting threat. As a result of this dichotomy, Margery's body is seen by McAvoy as "the site of conflict between opposed ideologies and conflicting desires"[35].

Scholars working within the fields of Gender Studies and Medieval Studies have rehabilitated *The Book of Margery Kempe*, effecting a totally changed perspective. In fact, there has been a shift from analysis of Margery, the persona of the narration, to that of Kempe the author of the text. As we shall be arguing, Margery Kempe has entered the 21st century as the polished authoress of her *Book*, managing to use all the narrative strategies available at that time, common to sub-genres like the Lives of the Saints and devotional treatises. The use of the concept of performance in the analysis of *The Book* has given back Kempe that agency she had been denied by readings based on gender stereotypes.

---

35 *Ibid.*, p. 126.

CHAPTER 1

Autobiography and Mystic Text[36]

In this chapter we shall be seeing how *The Book of Margery Kempe* reveals the figure of Margery Kempe as an upper middle-class woman from the late Middle Ages, whose written account of her mystical experience enabled her to establish an identity as a public figure. Margery establishes her image as the author of her book and gives it the function of *exemplum*. I intend to show how Margery uses *imitatio*, following the medieval literary tradition, in order to legitimize her authorial voice. She mentions and compares herself to other female mystics who also wrote about their spiritual experiences, or had them written down by their confessors; these mystics include Julian of Norwich and St. Bridget of Sweden, whose writings and fame were already well known in Kempe's day.

Thus Margery establishes her literary authority through the use of certain strategies in the composition of her book. She shows a considerable awareness of gender discrimination and lets it emerge through her words, in particular, during her encounters with adversaries representing both religious and political institutions[37]. The image of this woman as a public speaker emerging from such overt confrontations with the authorities is a result of the affirmation of

---

36 A version of this chapter previously appeared as "Margery and her Becoming Authoress", *Textus* 19, 2 (2006), pp. 323-338.
37 For an analysis of the metaphors and allegories used by Margery Kempe to represent authority, see A. Minnis, "Spiritualizing Marriage: Margery Kempe's Allegories of Female Authority", in *Translations of Authority in Medieval English Literature. Valuing the Vernacular* (Cambridge: Cambridge University Press, 2009), pp. 112-128.

her own agency within the domain of discourse; this is mainly, but not exclusively, the domain of the Word of God (which Margery publicly affirms as her own domain).

Margery is aware of the social norms that were used to silence women, but makes use of them by legitimizing herself through the figure of Christ, who asks her to pass on her visions and private "dalyawnce" with him.

With regard to textual and contextual elements, I shall aim to show how her book portrays a clever woman who applied her powers of speech and her knowledge with great determination, in order to legitimize her authorial voice, especially during the open confrontations with the finest and most powerful inquisitors, the official holders of the W/word. Margery Kempe was, in fact, accused of being a Lollard

"Þow xalt be brent, fals lollare." (Capitulum 13, Meech and Allen, p. 28)

"You shall be burnt, you false Lollard!" (Chap. 13, Windeatt, p. 64)

A particular reference is made to her habit of preaching in public, and Lollards actually acknowledged women's right to speak and teach the Word of Christ; however, because of her clever utilisation of the "word" and her knowledge of the Holy Writ, she constantly managed to dodge the stake.

In this way the image of the mystic becomes connected with that of a skilful *authoress:* an attentive observer, who was aware of the cultural, religious and socio-economic conditions of her time and who, despite claiming to be illiterate, was able to handle her knowledge of the (mainly religious) literary tradition[38].

---

38 For a challenging analysis on Margery Kempe's relation with the contemporary literary tradition see M. Furrow, "Unscholarly Latinity and Margery Kempe", in Toswell M. J. and E. M. Tyler (eds), *Studies in English Language and Literature: Doubt Wisely, Papers in Honour of E. G. Stanley* (London: Routledge, 1996), pp. 240-251.

Complexity and modernity

The *Book* presents the (spiritual) life of an English laywoman who lived between the end of the 14th century and the beginning of the 15th. As mentioned above, Margery was a burgess from King's Lynn in Norfolk and came from a well-known family of the town; her father, John Brunham, had several times been alderman and also mayor.

Using her experience as *exemplum*, Margery tells the story of her life beginning with her spiritual birth; she does it, on Christ's request, twenty years after her first vision, with the aid of a scribe (probably one of her sons) who was replaced by a scribe from the clergy after his death.

As we shall be seeing, Eva Figes's radio play *The True Tale of Margery Kempe* interestingly enough leaves the story and the words of the medieval mystic mostly unaltered.[39] Her work seems to be a mere dramatization of the *Book,* which, it has to be said, lays itself open to this sort of "media translation"; the visions described by Margery, and particularly those regarding the Passion and the Nativity of Christ and the Virgin Mary, (where Margery plays an active role), echo the scenes from medieval *mystery plays*.

Given Eva Figes's well known feminist commitment, and her attempt to give a voice to marginalised fictional characters,[40] one would have expected a reworking subverting the text; but on a careful reading of the *Book* one finds, as we shall be arguing in the final chapter, that Figes's interpretation of the text can be fully shared, because, if one considers the feminist views on the silenc-

---

[39] The main difference (at once manifest in the script) is that Figes places a particular stress on Margery's sexuality by inserting in the radio play "lovemaking sounds" in order to highlight the interplay of spirituality and sexuality in the *Book.*

[40] See, for instance, her *Nelly's Version* (1977), a rewriting of Emily Brontë's *Wuthering Heights*.

ing of women's voices in a patriarchal society, then the text is already a subversive one. Margery emerges as an empowered woman in medieval Christian society, and although it might be hazardous to speak of *ante litteram* feminism,[41] it is undeniable that, through her pointing out sexist discrimination, a certain gender awareness is present.

Margery's text raises a series of questions linked to its conception (literary genre, authorship, aim, and circulation), which make critical analysis highly controversial and have divided critics ever since the rediscovery of the manuscript in 1934[42].

Margery lived in an epoch of religious instability, and the text presents an unbalanced Catholic world, *threatened* by heresy. As stated above, Margery was several times accused of being a Lollard, a disciple of John Wycliffe. The wycliffite sect was critical of the clergy and proposed certain innovations in the religious life of lay people. They suggested that the Bible should be read in the vernacular and that it might be read privately. They also thought women should be able to preach in public and administer the sacraments.

When it was rediscovered and published by Hope Emily Allen in 1934, the *Book* was read as a mere historical document or as the confessional text of a peculiar mystic. However, the complexity of the figure of the protagonist and the peculiar aspects of her mysticism posed several problems of interpretation. The uncompromising and concrete figure that constantly emerged from the narrative was at variance with the models of mysticism in the Catholic tradition and exalted those material preoccupations that ill suited its icons of holiness. Cholmeley, for instance, maintains

---

41 A reading of the text as an example of early feminism is V. Neuburger, *Margery Kempe. A Study in Early English Feminism* (Berne, Berlin, New York: Peter Lang, 1994).

42 For a reconstruction of the different approaches to the *Book,* see S. Beckwith, "Problems of Authority in Late Medieval English Mysticism: Language, Agency, and Authority in *The Book of Margery Kempe*"; and G. Del Lungo Camiciotti, *Il libro di Margery Kempe.*

that some of the stories Margery tells are "unpalatable"[43] and because of her unsuitability in the eyes of the Church, Margery was also seen, and nearly *psycho-analysed*, as a hysteric[44].

This might be one of the reasons why all traces of the text were lost for so many centuries after its composition. Margery's name kept circulating, thanks to the purged version of Wynkyn de Worde (1501 c., which nevertheless contained only the more canonical passages of the text), but even so the *Book* disappeared for the five subsequent centuries.

These are examples of the different interpretations given to the *Book*: was Margery a hysteric or a real mystic? Was she, simply, a more or less pious woman with clear ideas on the *social* role of the Saints in the Catholic world?

As mentioned above, it was in 1934 that the only surviving manuscript of the work (London, British Library MS Additional 61823) was discovered in the possession of the Catholic Butler-Bowdon family[45]. This was probably a copy of the original and was signed by the amanuensis Salthows. On the manuscript are several annotations by monks from Mount Grace Priory (in Yorkshire); those in red ink, in particular, are evidence of the way the *Book* must have been used at the time that it was written. As Parsons suggests in her close study of the manuscript, "Carthusian

---

[43] K. Cholmeley, *Margery Kempe. Genius and Mystic* (London: Green & Co., 1947).

[44] See, for example, how clerics of the time judged her: J. McCAnn, "*The Book of Margery Kempe*", *Dublin Review,* 200 (1937), pp. 103-116; H. Thurston, "Margery the Astonishing", *The Month* 168 (1936), pp. 446-456. Hope Emily Allen herself charged Margery with accusations of fanaticism and neurosis in her preface to the 1940 edition. On the reception of the *Book* see B. Windeatt, "Introduction: Reading and Re-reading *The Book of Margery Kempe*", in J. H. Arnold and K. J. Lewis (eds), *A Companion to* The Book of Margery Kempe (Cambridge: D. S. Brewer, 2004), pp. 1-16.

[45] On the rediscovery of the manuscript, see H. Kelliher, "The Rediscovery of Margery Kempe: A Footnote", *The British Library Journal,* 22 (1996), pp. 259-263.

advisors" might have recommended the *Book* to women of the same social standing as Margery, because "a woman could particularly identify with the spiritual struggles and devotional practices of a married woman such as Margery, learning to emulate her successes and avoid her failures"[46].

It must be remembered that the female mystical tradition was, at the time, mostly of continental origin, and so a text in the vernacular (and therefore more easily circulated) relating the religious experience of a laywoman, who gave herself up tirelessly to prayer, pilgrimage and Samaritan life, (never forgetting her earthly occupations), might have had a more profound influence on English mothers and wives than an anchoress like Julian of Norwich. To a certain extent, Margery might seem a heroine in a novel, and her adventures might have been quite absorbing for her early readers.

Although the manuscript might lead us to suppose that the *Book* had a certain readership, there are no further traces of it after the suppression of Mount Grace Priory in 1539. Parsons believes that Salthows's manuscript must have been passed on to the Butler-Bowdons in order to rescue it from the destruction of Mount Grace[47].

It was mainly during the 1980s (and thereafter) that studies of *The Book of Margery Kempe* began to flourish, and in a new direction; this was mainly due to the previously-mentioned Gender Studies approaches to Medieval Studies and also to History and Economics[48].

---

46 K. Parsons, "The Red Ink Annotator of *The Book of Margery Kempe* and his Lay Audience", in Kerby-Fulton K. and M. Hilmo (eds), *The Medieval Professional Reader at Work: Evidence from Manuscripts of Chaucer, Langland, Kempe and Gower* (Victoria: ELS University of Victoria, 2001), p. 146.
47 *Ibid.*, p. 153.
48 See, for instance, D. Aers, *Community, Gender and Individual Identity. English Writing 1360-1430* and L. Staley Johnson, *Margery Kempe's Dissenting Fictions*.

The text began to be read as a product of the society from which it originated, i.e. a thriving English town, King's Lynn, a centre of international trade, where a mercantile mentality and economic preoccupations were part of everyday life and, therefore, not to be denied in the *education* of a woman of social standing such as Margery's[49]. As Aers points out,

> The mercantile world [...] was Margery's 'natural' and unquestioned element. [...] She had fourteen children. She herself was, for a time, an independent businesswoman, but gradually became as mobile as the fictional Wife of Bath or the figure of the poet in *Piers Plowman*, a pilgrim to Jerusalem and Europe, a visionary and a mystic[50].

These readings vouch for Margery's resolute personality, which surfaces more and more frequently as the narrative progresses. Margery seems an ambiguous figure, divided between her mysticism and her wish for public acknowledgement, between the private role of wife and the public one of mystic and prophetess, widely rebuked by most authorities at the time.

The complexity of this medieval text (and of its female authorial voice) is thus acknowledged; it throws up issues that are still argued over in contemporary literature, such as that of women's identity, and the influence of patriarchal society on the relaying of women's image. In Aers' words:

---

[49] A stimulating reconstruction of the historical and economical context in which *The Book of Margery Kempe* was written, with a particular focus on the mercantile town of King's Lynn is M. Gallyon, *Margery Kempe of Lynn and Medieval England* (Norwich: The Canterbury Press, 1995). On the social and economical context see also M. D. Myers, "A Fictional-True Self: Margery Kempe and the Social Reality of the Merchant Elite of King's Lynn", *Albion. A Quarterly Journal Concerned with British Studies*, 31, 3 (1999), pp. 377-394.

[50] D. Aers, *Community, Gender and Individual Identity. English Writing 1360-1430*, p. 73.

> [*The Book of Margery Kempe*] is one of the most fascinating English texts of the later Middle Ages, a precious work for anyone interested in the history of gender, subjectivities, and English culture. More than any other writing from this era, Margery Kempe's draws attention to many of the complex processes through which female identity might be made in a particular community and class. The *Book* resists conventional sublimations of such processes and the painful conflicts they entailed. This resistance makes it often an extremely moving text, after all these years, across the most thorough transformations of economic systems and mentalities. Thorough, undoubtedly, but perhaps less than total: could it be that at least some of her struggles resonate in our own domestic culture and have not been transcended?[51]

In analyses of medieval texts a gendered approach acquires ever greater importance, also in an attempt to rediscover a genealogy of women life-writers[52]. Smith, in particular, considers Margery a forerunner of women's autobiographical writing (placing her within the tradition created by Western feminist criticism, along with Margaret Cavendish, Charlotte Charke, Harriet Martineau and Maxime Hong Kingston). The main instrument for interpreting the text becomes the laying bare of those social mechanisms that determine the subaltern role of women within the family and actual society (and its representations). One might see in this unveiling the intentions of a woman writer determined to portray herself as an active character, not privately, but publicly, and by assuming different functions: above all that of communicating Christ's mes-

---

51 *Ibidem*.
52 On the rediscovery of life writing by women, see S. Benstock (ed.), *The Private Self. The Theory and Practice of Women's Autobiographical Writings* (London & New York: Routledge, 1988); D.C. Stanton (ed.), *The Female Autograph* (Chicago & London: The University of Chicago Press, 1984), with the above mentioned essay by J. M. Mueller, "Autobiography of a New 'Creatur': Female Spirituality, Selfhood, and Authorship in *The Book of Margery Kempe*" and S. Smith's volume *A Poetics of Women's Autobiography* (Bloomington. Indiana University Press, 1987), with her chapter "The Book of Margery Kempe: This Creature's Unsealed Life".

sage as authorizing voice. Against this background it is however important to show how Margery's encounters with lay and religious authorities were resolved through her "power of arguments"[53].

Strategies of legitimization

Tackling the question of literary authority and authorship in religious texts is always difficult and risky. The written word, in these texts, is always said to be inspired by an external, transcendent authority, which, in the Judaeo-Christian literary tradition, is that of Christ or the Godhead. This task becomes more complicated with regard to sacred texts written by holy women (especially mystics), whose literary authority is also mediated by institutionalized male control, whether by the legitimization of the Inquisition or by intervention on the texts by father confessors.

We shall be examining how *The Book of Margery Kempe* might be considered the result of the author's desire to reveal herself to the reading public. In the historical and social context of the epoch, to write of one's own experience meant negotiating an appropriate means of communication that might also be accepted by the Church. As one reads the *Book,* one notices that the author's awareness gradually increases, and that Margery uses her growing authority in order to oppose the members of political and ecclesiastical institutions (legitimate authorities, but not legitimized like her own authority).

Although the *Book* is a devotional treatise, if we analyse it as an early autobiography we also have to bear in mind the cultural and socio-economic background, so as not to deny the literary

---

53   L. Staley Johnson, *Margery Kempe's Dissenting Fictions.*

33

value of the book. One cannot, of course, say with certainty what Margery's intentions were when she set to work, but the text clearly shows signs of rebellion against corrupt institutions and a certain self-celebration, which might suggest that she herself chose to write down her story using God's authorization and the written tradition of other mystics, in order to give her book literary authority.

The strength of the *Book* seems to lie in the author's "powers of arguments"[54], in her interest in contemporary society and its ills, in all that stirs around her or, perhaps more pertinently, all that is stagnating.

Margery understands the role, among both religious and lay people, of the writings by mystics, and makes good use of it in legitimizing her own act of writing and the inherent attempt to claim her own subjectivity through the text, thus liberating herself from the shackles of her private roles of mother and wife.

Margery became acquainted with two different kinds of clergy. There were those confronting her, the corrupt ones, and the devout ones helping her on her way to holiness. Among the latter were those who read the Bible and hagiographic texts to Margery.

Kempe, though, creates a character that establishes a female subjectivity above and beyond the traditional family roles. Sheila Delany maintains that religion is for Margery a means of self-assertion:

> Religion is Margery's way of asserting her ownership of herself, of overcoming alienation while simultaneously providing the most poignant testimony to that alienation [...] One could also say that Margery discovered a way to use the system against the system – a way to leave home, travel, establish a name of herself, and meanwhile remain both chaste and respectable. Religion became her way of combating the special oppression of

---

54 *Ibidem.*

women, which she in no way understood as oppression, though she suffered and rebelled against its experiential weight[55].

Paradoxically though, Julia Long thinks that Margery affirms her subjectivity by denying herself through the authority of God:

> Kempe paradoxically gains a 'presence' through her own 'absence'. She is allowed a voice only inasmuch as she claims Christ is speaking through her. Her own presence is immaterial; she is legitimate only as a vessel of God[56].

Margery always seems to be struggling to define herself, to find the right path; in her psycho-analytical study, Long stresses Margery's courage in pursuing her self-realization:

> In the case of Margery Kempe, her vigorous striving for, and success in achieving, a subject position which is a refusal of the victim role comes across strongly in her autobiography. Given this, it seems to me that the [story of this woman stands as testimony to her] courage and to the possibility of negotiating forms of marginalisation in the struggle for subjectivity[57].

The Book of Margery Kempe presents a peculiar game of *authorizations*. Like any religious text, it follows a precise path: God reveals himself to a holy woman, redeems her from her sins and inspires her with holy words to be written down and passed on to other sinners awaiting salvation. Margery's mysticism responds to most of the characteristics of mystic speech described by De Certeau in *Heterologies* (1980), both in what he defines as *"modus loquendi"* and *"modus agendi"* and in the interplay of orthodoxy and heterodoxy. De Certeau explains in his essay that the centre of

---

55 S. Delany, "Sexual Economics", in Evans R. and L. Johnson (eds), *Feminist Readings in Middle English Literature. The Wife of Bath and All her Sect* (London and New York, Routledge: 1994), pp. 84-85.
56 J. Long, "Mysticism and Hysteria", in Evans R. and L. Johnson (eds), *Feminist Readings in Middle English Literature. The Wife of Bath and All her Sect*, p. 100.
57 *Ibid.*, pp. 107-108.

the text lies both within and without, because it is founded on God's Word and on the salvific role among sinners; he says:

> Divine utterance is both what founds the text, and what it must make manifest. That is why the text is destabilized: it is at the same time *beside* the authorized institution, but outside it and in what authorizes that institution, i.e. the Word of God[58].

Margery also displays a clear hierarchy in her *Book* (God-Saints-clergy-scribes-herself). This hierarchy consists of words legitimating her textual authority while being legitimated by extra-textual powers (such as God). I believe Margery is in control of this process and starts building it up from the very beginning of the *Book*.

She legitimizes her writing, by mentioning other representatives of the mystical written tradition who passed down their personal accounts; the Preface, written by the first scribe, also hints at this. In fact, the composition of the *Book* starts

> on þe day next aftyr Mary Maudelyn aftyr þe informacyon of þis creatur (Meech and Allen, p. 6)

> on the next day after Mary Magdalene, after the information of this creature (Windeatt, p. 38)

23rd July, as Del Lungo informs us, also corresponds to the day of St Bridget's death[59]. This is perhaps no accident. I personally think this is a narrative strategy adopted by Margery in order to give authority to her work. St Bridget and her book are often mentioned by Margery. On one particular occasion, Margery explicitly draws attention to the similarities in their mystical experiences and at the

---

58 M. De Certeau [1980], "Mystic Speech", in *Heterologies. Discourse on the Other*, English trans. by B. Massumi (Manchester: Manchester University Press, 1986), p. 92.

59 G. Del Lungo Camiciotti, *Il libro di Margery Kempe. Autobiografia spirituale di una laica del Quattrocento*, p. 110.

same time, through the words of Christ, legitimizes her writing doubly, as both literary and religious text. God, in fact, tells her:

> "For I telle þe forsoþe rygth as I spak to Seynt Bryde ryte so I speke to þe, dowtyr, & I telle þe trewly it is trewe euery word þat is wretyn in Brides boke, & be þe it xal be knowyn for very trewth." (Capitulum 20, Meech and Allen, p. 47)

> "For in truth I tell you, just as I spoke to St Bridget, just so I speak to you, daughter, and I tell you truly that every word that is written in Bridget's book is true, and through you shall be recognized as truth indeed." (Chap. 20, Windeatt, p. 83).

Apart from St Bridget, who Margery mentions again elsewhere, other mystics and mystical writings of the time appear in the text and lend authority to the *Book:*

> sum-tyme þe Secunde Persone in Trinyte; sumtyme alle thre Personys in Trinyte & o substawns in Godhede dalyid to hir sowle & informyd hir in hir feyth & in hys lofe how sche xuld lofe hym, worshepyn hym, & dredyn hym, so excellently þat sche herd neuyr boke, neyþyr Hyltons boke, ne [B]ridis boke, ne Stimulus Amoris, ne Incendium Amoris, ne non oþer þat euyr sche herd redyn þat spak so hyly of lofe of God but þat sche felt as hyly in werkyng in hit sowle yf sche cowd or ellys mygth a schewyd as sche felt. (Capitulum 17, Meech and Allen, p. 39)

> Sometimes the Second Person in Trinity, sometimes all Three Persons in Trinity and one substance in Godhead, spoke to her soul [...] so excellently that she never heard any book, neither Hilton's book, nor Bride's book, nor Stimulus Amoris, nor Incendium Amoris, nor any other book that she ever heard read, that spoke so exaltedly of the love of God as she felt working in her soul, if she could have communicated what she felt. (Chap. 17, Windeatt, p. 75)

Margery claimed to be illiterate, but her mention of those books and the style used in the narrative makes one think she was not. Near the beginning of the book when Margery tells of the accident that befell her in the church of St Margaret, she says

> [...] Sche knelyd up-on hir kneys, heldyng down hir hed and *hir boke in hir hand* [...]. (Capitulum 9, Meech and Allen, p. 21)

> [...] She knelt there, holding her head down, and *with her book in her hand* [...] (Chap. 9, Windeatt, p. 56)[60].

This might confirm the thesis that Margery was not *completely* illiterate but might have lacked Latin and so did not belong to "high culture". Also, speaking of style, Staley maintains (as previously mentioned) that the figure of the scribe is a trope lending further authority to the *Book*; personally, I do not adhere to this view, but I do agree with her when she says the influence of the scribes must have been somehow limited to that of amanuenses, a role which was, needless to say, common at the time[61].

As Del Lungo Camiciotti suggests in her ample introduction to the Italian version of the *Book,* the style of the narrative often takes on the tone of a biblical account and Margery's experiences of persecution are identified with Christ's Passion: her theatrical gestures recall those of the *mystery plays*[62].

Another aspect of Margery's (successful) attempt to lend authority to her holy status (and hence her *Book*) are her visits to renowned representatives of the clergy.

Her encounters with the Authorities are of two kinds: some Margery chooses to meet in order to ask for guidance and advice; others Margery is forced to meet when she is accused of heresy and, more covertly, of being socially disruptive.

Both types of meeting are successfully negotiated thanks to the woman's (and here again I borrow Staley's expression) "power

---

60 My italics.
61 L. Staley Johnson, "The Trope of the Scribe and the Question of Literary Authority in the Works of Julian of Norwich and Margery Kempe" and *Margery Kempe's Dissenting Fictions.*
62 Del Lungo Camiciotti, *Il libro di Margery Kempe. Autobiografia spirituale di una laica del Quattrocento.*

of arguments"[63]. Margery is always publicly acknowledged in the end as innocent and holy. All attempts at bringing evil upon her fail and fall back unfailingly on her persecutors, who, as a result of her "bold" speeches, are publicly exposed for their evil and corrupt behaviour. So when the Archbishop of York, who brings to mind Pontius Pilate ("What xal I don wyth hir?" – Meech and Allen, p. 125, "What shall I do with her?", Windeatt, p. 163), tells her that he has heard she is "a very wicked woman", she replies rather "boldly" (the narrative often underlines her answers during these encounters using this adverb):

> "Ser, so I her seyn þat ȝe arn a wikkyd man. And, ȝyf ȝe ben as wikkyd as men seyn, ȝe xal neuyr come in Heuyn les þan ȝe amende ȝow whil ȝe ben her." (Capitulum 52, Meech and Allen, p. 125)

> "Sir, I also hear it said that you are a wicked man. And if you are as wicked as people say, you will never get to heaven, unless you amend while you are here." (Chap. 52, Windeatt, p. 163)

Something else that surfaces from Margery's trials is her forceful subversion of gender roles. Accused of being a Lollard, she answers correctly to all the articles of faith, but her trials continue on a social level; the clerics advising the Archbishop of York tell him:

> "We knowyn wel þat sche can þe Articles of þe Feith, but we wil not suffyr hir to dwellyn a-mong vs, for þe pepil hath gret feyth in hir *dalyawnce*, | and perauentur sche myth peruertyn summe of hem." (*Ibidem*)

> We know very well that she knows the Articles of the Faith, but we will not allow her to dwell among us, because the people have faith in her *talk*, and perhaps she might lead some of them astray[64]. (*Ibidem*)

Margery is a threat to social order because most of her acts go against her gender (she speaks of holy matters and narrates tales

---

63   L. Staley Johnson, *Margery Kempe's Dissenting Fictions*.
64   My italics.

from the Bible), so she is overtly reproached for not adhering to a woman's role:

> So, as sche went forth to-Beuerloward wythþe seyd ȝemen & þe frerys beforn-seyd, þei mettyn many tymes wyth men of þe cuntre, whech seyd vn-to hir, "Damsel, forsake þis lyfe þat þu hast, & go spynne & carde as oþer women don, & suffyr not so meche schame & so meche wo." (Capitulum 53, Meech and Allen, p. 129)

> So as she went on towards Beverley with the said yeomen and the friars, they many times met with men of that district who said to her, "Woman, give up this life that you lead, and go and spin, and card wool as other women do, and do not suffer so much shame and so much unhappiness [...]." (Chap. 53, Windeatt, p. 168)

Margery continues speaking about the teachings of God and is accepted by several clerics, who recognize her holiness and wish to share in her experiences and learn about the word and message of God from her. Directly after the confrontation with the Archbishop of York, Margery appears to be even more fortified than previously by the awareness that she is recognised for her quick wits and her knowledge of the Holy Writ; she states this rather clearly and emphasises the intellectual level, repeatedly mentioning the authorization from God:

> Than sche, goyng a-ȝen to ȝorke, was receyued of mech pepil & of ful worthy clerkys, wheels enjoyed in owr Lord þat had ȝouyn hir not lettryd witte & wisdom to answeryn so many lernyd men wyth-owtyn velani or blame, thankyng be to God. (Capitulum 52, Meech and Allen, p. 128)

> Then she, going back again to York, was received by many people, and *by very worthy clerics,* who rejoiced in our Lord, who had given her – *uneducated as she was* – the *wit* and *wisdom* to answer so many *learned men* without shame or blame, thanks be to God[65]. (Chap. 52, Windeatt, p. 167)

---

65 My italics.

Not all issues arising from the text have been resolved and many themes have been left out of this analysis. Particularly interesting is the interplay of spirituality and sexuality in the text, the way in which Margery tells of her private "dalyawnce" with Christ. Her language shows the main characteristics of "mystic speech"; by mentioning them she demonstrates her knowledge of mystic texts, something which also emerges in the way she describes her divine communication with God as being like a fire burning her from the inside.

This is an issue that in the last fifteen/twenty years, in terms of rewriting, has triggered different responses at both a critical and a creative level. One of the latter is Eva Figes's previously-mentioned dramatization in *The True Tale of Margery Kempe;* another is Robert Glück's provocative novel *Margery Kempe*. Here Glück specifically draws on Margery's sexual peculiarity and creates a double narrative, interweaving her love for the young Christ (in one of the first chapters) to his love for a young man. This novel lends weight to the idea of Margery's *queerness*.

Her non-orthodox behaviour is also at the centre of Carolyn Dinshaw's *Getting Medieval*, a *queer* study stressing Margery's peculiar religious behaviour.

These re-workings of *The Book of Margery Kempe* contribute to the debate on the text, emphasising the physicality of the language used by Margery. The tale of the priest and the bear that she relates to the Archbishop of York, is meant (as we shall be seeing) to reveal his wickedness, and is a clear example of her language of the body, which in itself would merit a fuller study[66].

All these elements show *The Book of Margery Kempe* to be an extraordinary work that is not easy to interpret; its multilayered structure demands different perspectives of interpretation, and consequently many questions regarding the *Book* remain to be answered.

---

66 See chapter 52, Meech and Allen, pp. 126-127 and Windeatt, pp. 165-166.

Starting from the premise that this really is an early autobiography, I have shown the textual and contextual elements which have led me to believe that behind the text there lies a literary mind consciously making use of narrative strategies such as *imitation*, which were quite common at the time.

My analysis has restricted itself to the figure of Margery Kempe and to the strategies that she employs in order for her awareness as an author to emerge; she is not at all uneducated, but full of "witte & wisdom".

CHAPTER 2

Travels of/on Her Own[67]

The Book of Margery Kempe is an extraordinary source of information about not only the religious but also the historical and social contexts of Christian England between the 14th and the 15th century[68]. Contemporary readers have shown ever growing interest, especially when considering that *The Book of Margery Kempe* is one of the few surviving medieval English texts in which a woman relates accounts of her pilgrimages. Anthony Lutrell remarks that during the 14th century the number of women going on pilgrimages increased perceptibly; however by the time of the Crusades there had already been several cases of women who had gone to the Holy Land following their husbands to war, or even on their own[69].

---

67 A previous version of this chapter was published in Italian with the title "Margery Kempe: una mistica del Quattrocento in pellegrinaggio", *Fogli di anglistica*, 1, 1-2 (2007), pp. 83-91.
68 K. Ashley, "Historicizing Margery: *The Book of Margery Kempe* as Social Text", *The Journal of Medieval and Early Modern Studies*, 28, 2 (1998), pp. 371-389.
69 A. Lutrell, "Englishwomen as Pilgrims to Jerusalem: Isolda Parewastell, 1365", in Bolton Holloway J. et al. (eds), *Equally in God's Image: Women in the Middle Ages* (New York and Berne: Peter Lang), 1990, pp. 184-197. On medieval women pilgrims see also D. Webb, "Women Pilgrims of the Middle Ages", *History Today*, 48, 7 (1998), pp. 20-26.

Furthermore, Margery Kempe's text holds a central role in the English panorama not only because it contains a travel narrative written by a woman but also because it is written in the vernacular[70]:

> Women seldom left written accounts of their pilgrimages or wrote them in person. [...] For two centuries before Margery Kempe there is no surviving written account of an Englishwoman's pilgrimage to Jerusalem.[71]

Julia Bolton Holloway, Joan Bechtold and Constance Wright maintain in their introduction to *Equally in God's Image* (1990) that the pilgrimage gave those women who actually managed to go on a pilgrimage the right to speak to the higher ecclesiastical and civil authorities[72]. It is noticeable that each time Margery returns home from one of her pilgrimages, she willingly confronts these figures of authority demonstrating her eloquence and knowledge of the sacred texts with ever increasing boldness.

Margery Kempe sets out on journeys both in England and abroad in order to work on her spiritual development, or, more probably, in order to pursue a strategy of self-empowerment, through the narration of her mystical and religious experiences and the widespread circulation of her writings.

These are real pilgrimages: Margery visits the Holy Land, Assisi and Rome in the years 1413 and 1415, and in 1417 she goes to Santiago de Compostela[73]. A few years later, in 1433, Margery

---

70 Although *The Book of Margery Kempe* is one of the few existing documents on pilgrimages written by women and in the vernacular, C. Walker Bynum observes that many women wrote about their mystical experiences, or dictated their texts, in the vernacular.
71 *Ibidem*, pp. 184-185.
72 J. Bolton Holloway, J. Bechtold and C. Wright, "Introduction: The Body and the Book", in Bolton Holloway J. et al. (eds), *Equally in God's Image: Women in the Middle Ages* (New York and Berne: Peter Lang), 1990, pp. 1-23.
73 For a historical reconstruction of Kempe's pilgrimages see the "Suggested Chronology" in Barry Windeatt's edition of the *Book* (Harmondsworth: Penguin, 1985), and A. Goodman, *Margery Kempe and Her World*; in Italy,

accompanies her daughter-in-law, after the young woman has become a widow, to her native town, Dansk, and on the way back home Margery stops off to visit holy places such as Aachen[74].

The text also constitutes an important testimony to the "international relations" of the time, if we consider the more or less friendly contacts which the woman had during her pilgrimages with people from different countries: the Irish, the Germans, the Italians and the Saracens[75].

However, *The Book of Margery Kempe* cannot be considered as a travel narrative *tout court*. Margery's pilgrimages might be seen as an instrument of public legitimization of the figure of the mystic and are described merely from the spiritual point of view, the holy places visited provoking uncontrollable emotions and new and more intense visions in the woman. There are scarcely any details about the organization of the trips, about economic difficulties and the dangers encountered by a female pilgrim often travelling on her own, with an occasional "chance" male escort. It is not easy to find descriptions of the places that she visits, nor of the customs of the peoples with whom Margery comes into contact.

---

see also G. Del Lungo Camiciotti (ed.), *Il libro di Margery Kempe. Autobiografia spirituale di una laica del Quattrocento*.

74 She gives an account of her visit to Aachen in Book 2, chapter 7.

75 See Book 1, Chapter 30 of *The Book*. Goodman carefully reconstructs the historical context and explains that some of the choices made during Margery's journeys – such as longer stops or changes of routes – were probably due either to conflicts or to agreements between England and other countries in Northern Europe. The term "Saracens" used at Margery's time to speak about the Muslims who had fought against the Christians in the Crusades does not imply any negative connotation in her use of the term (when Margery went to the Holy Land the Crusades had been over for over a century). On the contrary, we shall be seeing that Kempe does not record any conflict between Christian pilgrims and the Muslims who receive them. The term Saracen in fact came to be used to indicate Arabs in general (see the *Oxford English Dictionary*).

The chapters that Margery devotes to narrating the time spent on pilgrimages abroad (from 26 to 43) serve to contribute to a greater legitimization of the figure of Margery as a devout woman and, mainly, as an orthodox Christian. It might also be possible to affirm that this lack of detailed description in the accounts of her pilgrimages is due to the long lapse of time between the actual journeys and the composition of the work (about twenty years), but it would probably be more appropriate to consider this as the result of a strategy which the author of the work clearly had in mind: she could enable her experiences to circulate among her contemporaries by endowing the narration with the hagiographic elements of an *exemplum,* aimed at the conversion of sinners. As previously mentioned, Parsons actually shows how the red ink annotations on the surviving manuscript indicate the presence of quite a wide readership[76].

Thus the accounts of her pilgrimages appear as a further tactic of self-legitimization, both as regards her first journey in England and her brave crossing of Europe with Jerusalem as her final destination. This is not only another way of explicitly following in the footsteps of saints like Saint Bridget, who had gone on pilgrimages before her, but is also a way of silencing accusations of Lollardy; the followers of John Wycliffe in fact denounced such religious practices (the charges of heresy started when Margery was "visited" by public manifestations of weeping and despair during her travels around England)[77].

What might be more interesting in the examination of Margery's pilgrimages is the role of her various encounters in the course of her travels and how they might validate Margery's im-

---

[76] K. Parsons, "The Red Ink Annotator of *The Book of Margery Kempe* and his Lay Audience".

[77] On Margery's identification with other female saints, see G. Gibson McMurray, "St. Margery: *The Book of Margery Kempe*", in Bolton Holloway J. *et al.* (eds), *Equally in God's Image: Women in the Middle Ages* (New York and Berne: Peter Lang, 1990), pp. 144-163.

age as a public figure and a socially influential one (and not only at a religious level). Margery uses the descriptions of her meetings with foreign people as legitimization of her faith and consequently of her person, in open contraposition with the unwelcoming reception which Margery received from her English travel companions. In chapter 30, we read:

> And þe Frerys of þe Tempyl mad hir gret cher and ȝouyn hir many gret relykys, desiryng þat sche schuld a dwellyd stille a-mongs hem, ȝyf sche had wold, for þe feyth þei had in hir. Also þe Saraȝines mad mych of hir & conueyd hir & leddyn hir abowtyn in þe cuntre whet sche wold gon. & sche fond alle pepyl good on-to hir & gentyl saf only hit owyn cuntremen. (Capitulum 30, Meech and Allen, p. 75)

> And the friars of the Church of the Holy Sepulchre were very welcoming to her and gave her many great relics, wanting her to remain among them if she had wished, because of the belief they had in her. The Saracens also made much of her, and conveyed and escorted her about the country wherever she wanted to go. And she found all people good and gentle to her, except her own countrymen. (Chap. 30, Windeatt, p. 111)

The way in which the Arabs are said to receive Margery is rather interesting in that they are described in more than one passage as peaceful and friendly. The last crusade ended in 1291, and although the references to the Saracens are brief and not very detailed, *The Book of Margery Kempe* becomes a precious testimony to the contacts between the western and eastern worlds and the historical and political climate of the time.

The frequent positive comments regarding foreigners' benevolence towards Margery, in both the Holy Land and Rome (as well as in Venice), are at variance with the scorn and isolation she receives from her compatriots. Both attitudes are a consequence of her behaviour following Christ's revelations and her subsequent experiences of insistent weeping.

It is often her friendship with foreign priests which enables her to be re-admitted among her fellow travellers, tired of the physical manifestations of her faith and of her constant talk about the Gospels. The words of some of the people that Margery meets show how the fame of this devoted woman was spreading quickly both in England and in the countries she visited; for instance, in Rome, the English friars at the Hospital of Saint Thomas accepted her in their midst after initially refusing her, when they

> [...] herd tellyn what lofe & what fauowr sche had in þe cyte [...]. (Capitulum 39, Meech and Allen, p. 94)

> [...] heard tell of what love and favour she had in the city [...]. (Chap. 39, Windeatt, p. 131)

From Lynn to the Holy Land via Italy

The first pilgrimages that Margery undertook differed from later ones, not only because of the distance and the duration, but because of their differing aims and results. Escorted by her husband, in 1413 Margery had several important encounters in England with ecclesiastical authorities, including meetings with the Archbishop of Lincoln, Philip Repyngdon, and with the Archbishop of Canterbury, Thomas Arundel[78]. These are of considerable importance when determining Margery's personality, and not only her orthodoxy but also the influence she exercised on her listeners through her "power of arguments". Just as crucial as these contacts, for the public validation of Margery's mystic experiences, was her visit to the renowned contemporary anchoress Dame Julian in Norwich, who was already famous because of her

---

[78] See chapter 15 for the meeting with the Archbishop of Lincoln and chapter 16 for the meeting with the Archbishop of Canterbury.

works[79]. Proof of this lies in the fact that the author gives ample coverage to the holy conversation and in particular to Julian's words on the grace of "co*m*pu*n*ccyon, contricyon, swetnesse & deuocyon, co*m*passyon w*yth* holy meditacyon & hy co*n*templacyon" ("compunction, contrition, sweetness and devotion, compassion with holy meditation and high contemplation")[80] that God placed in Margery's soul:

> þe ankres wan expert in swech thyng*ys* & good cownsel cowd ʒeuyn. Þe ankres, hery*ng* þe me*r*uelyows goodness of owyr Lord, hyly thankyd God w*yth* al hir hert for hys visitacyon, cownselyng þis creatur to be obedyent to þe wyl of owyr Lord God & fulfyllyn w*yth* al hir mygthys what-euy*r* he put in hir sowle yf it wer not a-geyn þe worshep of God & p*ro*fyte of hir euyn-cr*is*ten. (Capitulum 18, Meech and Allen, p. 42)
>
> [...] the anchoress was expert in such things and could give good advice. The anchoress, hearing the marvellous goodness of our Lord, highly thanked God with all her heart for his visitation, advising this creature to be obedient to the will of our Lord and fulfil with all her might whatever he put into her soul, if it were not against the worship of God and the profit of her fellow Christians. (Chap. 18, Windeatt, p. 78)

Julian of Norwich encourages Margery to follow on the way of devotion and her discourse places Margery firmly in the tradition of female saints (and specifically of the mystics) who devoted themselves to writing and to the spreading of Christ's revelations. Through these words, Julian implicitly gives her approval to Margery to use her life as *exemplum* for the edification of other Christians. In the same way, in spite of her social role as wife and mother, Saint Bridget, whom Margery very often mentions, had also devoted her life to contemplation. Besides, Julian justifies Margery's manifestations of uncontrollable weeping and thus con-

---

79 The encounter and conversation with Julian of Norwich is recorded in chapter 18.
80 Meech and Allen, p. 42; Windeatt, p. 77.

tributes to the rejection of charges that she might have been prey to the devil's influence:

> [...] whan God visyteth a creatur wyth terys of contrisyon, deuosyon, er compassyon, he may & owyth to leuyn þat þe Holy Gost is in hys sowle. Seynt Powyl seyth þat þe Holy Gost askyth for vs wyth mornynggys & wepyngys vnspekable, þat is to seyn, he makyth vs to askyn & preyn wyth mornynggys & wepyngys so plentyvowsly þat þe terys may not be now-meryd. Ther may non euyl spyrit ʒeuyn þes tokenys, for Ierom seyth þat terys turmentyn mor þe Devylle þan don þe peynes of Helle. (Capitulum 18, Meech and Allen, pp. 42-43)

> [...] when God visits a creature with tears of contrition, devotion or compassion, he may and ought to believe that the Holy Ghost is in his soul. St. Paul says that the Holy Ghost asks for us with mourning and weeping unspeakable; that is to say, he causes us to ask and pray with mourning and weeping so plentifully that the tears may not be numbered. No evil spirit may give these tokens, for St. Jerome says that tears torment the devil more than do the pains of hell. (Chap. 18, Windeatt, p. 78)

The contacts with the ecclesiastical authorities can be considered as preparatory to her pilgrimage to the Holy Land, which (carried out upon Christ's direct exhortation) Margery sees not as a penance but as a reward for her devotion. As we shall see, her requests to the Archbishops aim, on the one hand, to validate her new life-style and, on the other, to legitimize her autonomy from her husband at the social level, through the authorization of the Church. Thus, her emancipation from the conjugal knot is sealed by the public emblems of chastity:

> And þan sche seyd ferþermor, "My Lord, yf it lyke ʒow, I am comawndyd in my sowle þat ʒe schal ʒyue me þe mantyl & þe ryng & clothyn me al in whygth clothys. And, yf ʒe clothyn me in erth, owyr Lord Ihesu Cryst xal clothyn ʒow in Heuyn, as I vndyrstond be reuelacyon." (Capitulum 15, Meech and Allen, p. 34)

> And then she said furthermore, "My Lord, if it please you, I am commanded in my soul that you shall give me the mantle and the ring, and clothe me all

in white clothes. And if you clothe me on earth, our Lord Jesus Christ shall clothe you in heaven, as I understand through revelation". (Chap. 15, Windeatt, p. 69)

Margery goes to see the Archbishop of Lincoln to ask for permission to dress in white and wear the ring as symbols of her chaste union with Christ. The Archbishop of Lincoln is a sympathizer of Margery's mysticism (and had been a follower of Wycliffe in his youth), but although he is given leave by her husband, John Kempe, to grant her the white robes and the ring, he asks them to visit to the Archbishop of Canterbury, thus underlining the necessity to officialize those choices of Margery's which might have appeared rather unorthodox at the time of Lollardism.

As a matter of fact, although *The Book* includes a long conversation with Thomas Arundel, the Archbishop of Canterbury, who gives her permission to receive weekly Holy Communion and to choose her own confessor, she is nonetheless not welcomed by the rest of the clergy in Canterbury and is finally accused of heresy and forced to leave the town in haste.

All these sufferings and tribulations are narrated as necessary obstacles for her spiritual growth, and at the same time, they force Margery to search for new strategies of legitimization. Apart from simply demonstrating her orthodoxy and, more specifically, her distancing from sects such as the wycliffites (lollards were against such practices), the pilgrimage was a good way of obtaining indulgences, as the text shows:

> And so sche wan w*yth* gret deuocyon, w*yth* plentevows teerys, & wyth boystows sobbyng*ys*, for in þis place is plen*yr* remyssyon. & so in in oþ*er* iiij placys in þe Tempyl. On is in þe Mownt of Caluarye; an-oþ*er* at þe gr*a*ue whet owyr Lord was berijd; þe thridde is at þe marbyl ston þ*at*. hys *pre*ciows body was leyd on whan it was takyn of þe cros; þe ferd in þ*er* þe holy cros was berijd, & in many oþer placys of Ierusalem. (Capitulum 29, Meech and Allen, p. 72)

51

> And so she was with great devotion, with plenteous tears, and with violent sobbing, for in this place there is plenary remission, and so there is in four other places in the Church of the Holy Sepulchre. One is on the Mount Calvary; another at the grave where our Lord was buried; the third is at the marble stone that his precious body was laid on when it was taken from the cross; the fourth is where the holy cross was buried; and in many other places of Jerusalem. (Chap. 29, Windeatt, p. 108)

This practice is well documented in other texts, written shortly after *The Book of Margery Kempe*, such as the one by the Dominican friar Felix Fabri, entitled *The Book of Wanderings*, which describes in detail two journeys he undertook to the Holy Land in the 1480s[81]. Fabri's text does not only focus on the preparations for his journeys and on the overland travels which precede the actual voyage to the Holy Land (ships usually docked in Jaffa), but also destines much space to the description of the places they visit. Goodman makes reference to the existence of travel books for pilgrims, which reported the number of indulgences to be gained at each shrine and holy place visited by the pilgrim[82]. He uses *The Book of Wanderings* to reconstruct Margery's routes. After publicly paying off all her debts and those of her husband, she travels to Yarmouth where she embarks for Zierikzee (in the Netherlands) with her maid and a group of pilgrims and they then continue their journey to Constance (in Germany). Goodman remarks that in England it was mostly representatives of the clergy and the nobility who went on pilgrimages; however, he also observes that there were sometimes women from the lower classes among the pilgrims (the "common folk")[83].

In Constance, Margery is abandoned by her fellow pilgrims because she refuses to conform to their behaviour, i.e. she refuses to eat meat and drink wine and keeps quoting from the sacred texts

---

[81] I am grateful to Professor Elio Di Piazza for bringing to my attention Felix Fabri and his work.
[82] A. Goodman, *Margery Kempe and Her World*, pp. 152-153.
[83] *Ibidem*.

and speaking about God's revelations. The other pilgrims are also extremely vexed by her continuous tears of compunction:

> The company was wroth & in gret angyr. Þei ȝouyn hir ouyr to þe legate & seyden vttyrly þei woldyn no mor medyl wyth hir. He ful benyngly & goodly receyued hir as þow sche had ben hys modyr & receyued hir golde a-bowte xx pownd, & ȝet on of hem wythhelde wrongfully a-bowte xvj pownd. & þei wythheldyn also hir mayden & wolde not letyn hir gon wyth hir maystres, not-wythstondyng sche had behestyd hir maystres & sekyrd hir þat sche xulde not forsake hir for no nede. And þe legate ordeyned for þis creatur & made hir chawnge as sche had ben hys modyr. (Capitulum 27, Meech and Allen, p. 64)

> The company was extremely angry. They gave her over to the legate and said absolutely that they would have nothing more to do with her. He very kindly and benevolently received her as though she had been his mother, and took charge of her money – about twenty pounds – and yet one of them wrongfully withheld about sixteen pounds. And they also withheld her maid-servant and would not let her go with her mistress, notwithstanding that she had promised her mistress and assured her that she would not forsake her for any necessity. And the legate made all arrangements for this creature (and organized for her the exchange of her English money into foreign money), as though she had been his mother. (Chapter 27, Windeatt, p. 100)

This excerpt gives quite interesting, if only marginal, information about practical questions and the habits of the pilgrims. The task of exchanging money was usually assigned to one of the pilgrims, who was probably also in charge of looking after the money of his fellow pilgrims.

Belonging to the upper middle classes, the daughter of a well-known alderman of Lynn, Margery is constantly anxious about having a travelling companion with her; when her husband stays behind in England, as is the case with her pilgrimage to the Holy Land, she takes with her a maidservant.

The above-mentioned episode, with Margery abandoned by her countrymen and especially by her own maid, underlines the implicit comparison between herself and Christ, who was betrayed and forsaken by his most cherished disciples. Pilgrimage, as Bolton Holloway, Bechtold and Wright remark, also responded to the need to give prominence to the imitation of the life of the saint whose shrine or relics were being visited; for those like Margery, who went to the Holy Land it might well be Christ himself that was emulated. As mentioned above, according to several scholars interested in pilgrimage accounts (Bolton Holloway, Bechtold and Wright among them), it was quite common for pilgrims to take with them a copy of the Bible and specific travel-guides for pilgrims, and so it might appear rather odd that Margery did not take any of these with her nor even mention them. Margery, however, kept quoting from the Gospels in public which lends further weight to the author's choice of publicly confirming her profound knowledge of the sacred texts. It might have been precisely this insistence on the centrality of her person – as interpreter and strict follower of the Gospels – that induced her fellow pilgrims to repeatedly exclude her from communal moments until her categorical final exclusion.

Through the intervention of divine providence, however, the woman is guided and chaperoned by an old man, called William, who escorts her to Bologna and then to Venice, a port of departure for ships headed for the Holy Land (as Fabri's text confirms[84]).

Of all this exhausting movements across Europe, Margery does not utter a single word. She merely describes her relationship with her travelling companions, and only briefly dwells on her hosts and the mainly benevolent welcome she receives abroad. Goodman stresses that the inhabitants of places like Venice probably profited economically from the passage of pilgrims through their city, since these often had to stay for many weeks before they could actually set sail for the Holy Land (normally in spring or in summer); it was therefore likely that pilgrims were treated with respect and kindness.

---

84 See A. Stewart (ed.), *The Book of the Wanderings of Brother Felix Fabri* (Palestine Pilgrim's Text Society, London, 1892-1893).

Margery must have arrived in Venice much earlier than spring or summer, presumably between the end of 1413 and the beginning of 1414[85].

As regards her stay in Venice, she simply describes the preparations for the sea voyage, the arrangement of bedding and the goods she would need on board ship. She also adds that after making all her preparations she had decided not to embark on the first available ship (on which her former fellow pilgrims were to embark), since the Lord had shown her in a vision that it would not be a safe crossing. The other English pilgrims believe this prophecy, which serves to raise their esteem for Margery, whom they then follow on board a second ship.

Although the total lack of description of Venice and its city-life might be surprising, Goodman believes that this might also be due to the pomp and ostentation of the religious processions (frequent in that period, according to the historian), which did not become her book's tone of pious devotion, nor the figure of an orthodox mystic[86].

The readers are not given any particulars about the voyage to Jaffa, other than Margery saying that it was untroubled and uneventful, thus confirming her decision to change ship.

The places she visits in the Holy Land – Jerusalem, the Holy Sepulchre, the Mount of Calvary, Mount Zion, Bethlehem, the River Jordan and Bethany – all stir emotions in her which intensify her love for the human figure of Christ until she finally identifies completely with him in mystical union. Of these sites, it is only the emotive impact on Margery which is recorded; there is no description of scenery or towns.

---

85 See B. Windeatt, "Suggested Chronology"in *The Book of Margery Kempe*; A. Goodman, *Margery Kempe and Her World*, and G. Del Lungo Camiciotti (ed.), *Il libro di Margery Kempe. Autobiografia spirituale di una laica del Quattrocento*.
86 A. Goodman, *Margery Kempe and Her World*.

On the one hand then, Margery's pilgrimage has as its explicit aim her spiritual growth: the words of God reassure Margery regarding the nature of her journey; God has invited her to visit the places where Christ had lived to reward her faith in him, not to forgive her sins (which had already been forgiven). On the other hand, the account of her visits to these same places, given her devotion, the welcome afforded by the Franciscan friars and the Saracens, has as its aim the public affirmation of Margery as an orthodox mystic, a figure to command respect and attention[87].

As confirmation of Margery's spiritual development, on her return from Jerusalem, Margery spends a long time in Italy, firstly in Assisi and then several weeks in Rome, where her time is spent caring for the poor and the weak rather than in pilgrimage. Margery only visits a few shrines and churches, and instead, upon the request of one of the friars whom she meets in Rome, she devotes her time to assisting a poor woman. Her new comportment serves to show how the visit to the Holy Land has affected Margery positively; the sojourn in the land where Christ lived has inspired her to live a life of total devotion to her fellow man, in imitation of Christ. In Rome, Margery is portrayed as God's servant; by describing herself as humble and at the service of the poor, ridding herself of the little money she still possessed, Margery shows how her conversion has now been fully accomplished.

Apart from having the merit of emphasising, though fleetingly, the relationship between Christians and Muslims in the Holy Land at the beginning of the 15th century, the part of the narrative dealing with her pilgrimages has a precise objective. Her identification with Christ, finalised in the Holy Land, does not

---

[87] See N. K. Yoshikawa, "The Jerusalem Pilgrimage: The Centre of the Structure of the *Book of Margery Kempe*", *English Studies. A Journal of English Language and Literature*, 86, 3 (2005), pp. 193-205 and also her "Searching for the Image of New Ecclesia: Margery Kempe's Spiritual Pilgrimage Reconsidered", *Medieval Perspectives*, 11 (1996), pp. 125-138.

only legitimate Margery through the revelations of Christ, but also has the function of giving Margery the right to speak in public.

Her flight from Canterbury, in order to escape the accusation of heresy, after her meeting with the Archbishop Arundel, is forgotten once she is back from her pilgrimage to the Holy Land. The encounters which follow, both with the Mayor of Leicester and the Archbishop of York, depict a new Margery, now endowed with agency. She is now able to respond correctly and artfully to the fresh accusations of heresy; this process of self-legitimization is surprising in a book dating back to the 15th century.

CHAPTER 3

Abjection and the Body

The Book of Margery Kempe presents a continuous crossing of borders, constituted by social conventions and expectations, but also by physical and moral boundaries. Margery's public discourses, and especially the stories that she tells – which are more than once real *exempla* – often focus on the relationship with the body and sexuality, though this is not always explicitly stated[88]. When Margery describes the physical manifestations of Christ's visitations and the contrition on her body, and when she tells stories about the immorality of the clergy, the stress is on bodily functions, i.e. the emission of bodily substances whilst weeping, vomiting, excreting; these actually prove to be disturbing (at least for contemporary readers) in a text dealing with love for God. Many questions arise about the representation of physicality and about what Julia Kristeva has defined in terms of abjection[89].

Drawing on Mary Douglas's theoretical positions in *Purity and Danger* (1966)[90], Judith Butler observes that the body as conveyer of values is a concept constructed and shaped historically in order to maintain a stable, regulated social order:

---

[88] On the role of the *exempla* told in *The Book of Margery Kempe* and the cultural influence of such texts, see C. Ho, "Margery Reads Exempla", *Medieval Perspectives* (1993), pp. 143-152.
[89] J. Kristeva (1980), *Powers of Horror. An Essay on Abjection*, English trans. by L. S. Roudiez (New York: Columbia University Press, 1982).
[90] M. Douglas (1966), *Purity and Danger. An Analysis of Concept of Pollution and Taboo* (London and New York: Routledge, 2002).

> Any discourse that establishes the boundaries of the body serves the purpose of instating and naturalizing certain taboos regarding the appropriate limits, postures, and modes of exchange that define what it is that constitutes bodies [...].[91]

The body (the gendered body in particular) is one of the aspects which, though not central, emerge insistently in *The Book of Margery Kempe*. The text describes a continuous shift of the boundaries of the body, raising questions about the medieval discourses on physicality. In Christian visual and literary representations, the body has often been depicted as the temporary carnal (more than simply physical) "house" of the soul, the prison of the soul. At the same time, however, if we focus on the hagiographic representation of physicality, for Christian saints the body is an instrument allowing the imitation through suffering of the life of Christ. In the words of Caroline Walker Bynum:

> Control, discipline, even torture of the flesh is, in medieval devotion, not so much the rejection of physicality as the elevation of it – a horrible yet delicious elevation – into a means of access to the divine[92].

Walker Bynum remarks that both in paintings and in hagiographic texts, the tortured and suffering bodies of the saints are directly linked to Christ, often through what she calls "holy exuding", with, for instance, bleeding stigmata or lactating breasts (a maternal image of nurturing which was also surprisingly associated with Christ)[93]. Walker Bynum maintains that in the period from the 13th

---

91 J. Butler, *Gender Trouble*, p. 166. On the body in medieval literature see W. Harding, "Body into Text: *The Book of Margery Kempe*", in Lomperis I. and S. Stanbury (eds), *Feminist Approaches to the Body in Medieval Literature* (Philadelphia: University of Pennsylvania Press, 1993), pp. 168-187.
92 C. Walker Bynum, "The Female Body and Religious Practice in the Later Middle Ages", p. 182.
93 In addition to C. Walker Bynum "The Female Body and Religious Practice in the Later Middle Ages" (in particular, pp. 206-213), see also her specific

century to the 16th century the body assumed a new religious significance and female spirituality was characterised by a strong presence of the body in mystical phenomena and devotional writing. Moreover, she argues that this peculiarity of female spirituality was directly connected to the idea, promoted by both philosophers and theologians, that "the female" was associated with "the fleshly"[94]. On the other hand, Walker Bynum agrees that physicality and spirituality were closely linked by a new concept of the person as "psychosomatic unity"[95].

The Book of Margery Kempe makes use of such images and sensual language in its descriptions of mystical encounters with Christ. This was common in medieval devotional texts, transmitting many of the Christian values; however in Margery Kempe's text some of these images of bodily border-crossing, through textual elements, are aimed at dismantling the "fictions of power". Once she has received authorization from the Archbishop of York and the Archbishop of Canterbury, and completed her spiritual development through her pilgrimage to the Holy Land and Italy, Kempe, in her subsequent encounters, makes use of distasteful descriptions of foul bodies as metaphors of immorality. As we shall be seeing, such tales of defilement as "The priest and the pear-tree" are aimed at overtly criticising certain representatives of the Church. At the same time, when relating episodes such as that of the sea voyage from Calais with the widow from London, Kempe subverts the relationship between the abject and those who reject the abject.

---

volume *Jesus as Mother* (Berkeley, Los Angeles and London: University of California Press, 1982).
94 C. Walker Bynum, "The Female Body and Religious Practice in the Later Middle Ages", p. 183.
95 *Ibidem.*

Gender and *queer* performances

In the last chapter of *Gender Trouble* (1990), "Subversive Bodily Acts", Judith Butler explores some of the works by the most influential theorists contributing to the debate on gender and sexuality: Simone de Beauvoir, Julia Kristeva, Michel Foucault and Monique Wittig. Butler maintains that the identity of gender is not an *a priori* set of attributes related to a determined sex but a cultural construct; it is not a fact, an immanent "truth", but an idea created through the repetition of determined acts and gestures which have been historically filled with conventional "gendered" meanings; gender is hence seen as *cultural fiction*[96].

These acts are patterns with historically determined regulations upon which the collectivity agrees. Every member of society is expected to conform to these norms or else be rejected as *abject*. If identity is the enactment of these series of actions, we might argue that not only does Margery make use of the language of physicality to follow in the tradition of medieval female devotion, but she even shapes her place in society by playing with the concept of abjection. Through the *exempla* that she relates and through the narration of her encounters with scornful people who spurn her, Margery puts into practice a series of acts of resistance. Although they place her beyond the bounds of social convention, they do bring her closer to sanctification, and hence place her at the centre of narration of holiness and religious society itself. Gender, then, is not sufficient when describing Margery's identity, since there emerges a conflict between her social functions as wife and mother and her enactments of virginity.

The body is the means through which her identity seeks affirmation, through the repetition of acts, constructing different "styles of the flesh", as Butler calls these gendered public (or

---

[96]   J. Butler, *Gender Trouble*, pp. 101-180.

"dramatic") actions, which generate identity conflicts in Margery's narrative. Margery is constantly trying to make her sexual role clear; she is worried about her chastity (which is actually the result of performative acts) and feels it is continuously under threat. For instance, when the Mayor of Leicester, not content with her defence, orders the jailer to put her into prison, her preoccupation is with her (regained) purity:

> The jaylerys man, hauyng compassyon of hir wyth wepyng terys, seyd to þe Meyr, "Ser, I haue non hows to put hir inne les þan I putte hir a-mong men". Þan sche, meuyd wyth compassyon of man whech had compassyon of hir preyng for grace & mercy to þat man as to hir owyn sowle, seyd to þe Meyr, "I prey ʒow, ser, put me not a-mong men, þat I may kepyn my chastite & my bond of wedlak to myn husbond, as I am bowndyn to do." [...] Than þe Styward of Leycetyr, a semly man, sent for þe seyd creatur to þe jaylerys wyfe, & sche, for hir husband was not at hom, wolde not late hir gon to no man, Styward ne oþer. (Capitulum 46, 47, Meech and Allen, pp. 111, 112)

> The gaoler's man, having compassion for her with weeping tears, said to the Mayor, "Sir, I have no place to put her in, unless I put her in among men."
> Then she – moved with compassion for the man who had compassion for her, praying for grace and mercy for that man as to her own soul – said to the Mayor, "I beg you, sir, not to put me among men, so that I may keep my chastity, and my bond of wedlock to my husband, as I am bound to do." [...] Then the Steward of Leicester, a good-looking man, sent for the said creature to the gaoler's wife, and she – because her husband was not at home – would not let her go to any man, Steward or otherwise. (Chapters 46, 47, Windeatt, pp. 149, 150)

At the same time she realises that as a married woman she is required to conform to the norm. When the Mayor of Leicester subjects Margery to examination by holy clerks, they find that she cannot be denigrated with regard to religious aspects because she is very familiar with the articles of the faith:

> & so sche answeryd forth to alle þe artycles as many as þei wolde askyn hir þat þei wer wel plesyd, Þe Meyr, whech was hir dedly enmy, he seyd, "In

> fayth, sche menyth not *wyth* hir hert as sche seyth with hir mowthe." And þe clerkys seyden to hym, "Sir, sche answeryth | ryth wel to vs." (Capitulum 48, Meech and Allen, p. 115)

> And so she went on answering on all the articles, as many as they wished to ask her, so that they were well pleased.
> The Mayor, who was her deadly enemy, said, "Truly, she does not mean with her heart what she says with her mouth."
> And the clerics said to him, "Sir, she answers us very well." (Chap. 48, Windeatt, p. 153)

The mayor can only point a finger at the sexual and social threat represented by a married woman, and preacher, dressed in white (a symbol of virginity), travelling around on her own. It is interesting to observe how Margery does not report the mayor's actual words, merely describing them as "rep*r*euows" ("reproving") and "vngoodly" ("indecent"), hinting at the possible sexual nature of his reproaches and accusations:

> Þan þe Meyr alto-rebukyd hir & rehersyd many rep*r*euows word*y*s & vngoodly, þe whiche is mor expedient to be co*n*celyd þa*n* expressyd. "Sir," sche seyde, "I take witnesse of my Lord Ihesu Crist, whos body is her p*r*esent in þe Sacrament of þe Awter, þa*t* I neu*y*r had part of mannys body in þis worlde in actual dede be wey of synne, but of myn husbond*y*s body, whom I am bowndyn to be þe lawe of mat*r*imony, & be whom I haue born xiiij childeryn." (Capitulum 48, Meech and Allen, p. 115)

> Then the Mayor severely rebuked her and repeated many reproving and indecent words, which it is more fitting to conceal than express.
> "Sir," she said, "I take witness of my Lord Jesus Christ, whose body is here present in the sacrament of the altar, that I never had part of any man's body in this world in actual deed by way of sin, except my husband's body, to whom I am bound by the law of matrimony, and by whom I have borne fourteen children". (Chap. 48, Windeatt, p. 153)

Margery is so well aware of the role of women in patriarchal society that she draws the mayor's attention to her husband and fourteen children, thus making it clear that she has complied fully with her maternal duties. Her "lawful" status is further legitimated by the authorization of God, here described as husband:

> "For I do ȝow to wetyn, ser, þat þer is no man in þis worlde þat I lofe so meche as God, for I lofe hym a-bouyn al thynge, &, ser, I telle ȝow trewly I lofe al men in God & for God." (Capitulum 48, Meech and Allen, p. 115)

> "For I would have you know, sir, that there is no man in this world that I love so much as God, for I love him above all things, and, sir, I tell you truly, I love all men in God and for God." (Chap. 48, Windeatt, p. 153)

Margery goes one step further and overturns the sexual accusations by making a veiled, and somehow menacing, allegation of homosexuality to the mayor, who, in reply, can only point at her white clothes, a symbol of the social and sexual disruption of the Lollards:

> Also ferþermor sche seyd pleynly to hys owyn persone, "Sir, ȝe arn not worthy to ben a meyr, & þat xal I preuyn be Holy Writte, for owr Lord God seyde hym-self er he wolde takyn veniawnce on þe cyteys, 'I xal comyn down & seen,' & ȝet he knew al thyng. & þat was not ellys sir, but for to schewe men as ȝe ben þat ȝe schulde don non execucyon in ponischyng but ȝyf ȝe had knowing be-forn þat it wer worthy for to be don. &, syr, ȝe han do al þe contrary to me þis day, for, syr, ȝe han cawsyd me myche despite for thyng þat I am not gilty in. I pray God for-ȝeue ȝow it." (Capitulum 48, Meech and Allen, p. 116)

> Also furthermore she said plainly to his face, "Sir, you are not worthy to be a mayor, and that shall I prove by Holy Writ, for our Lord God said himself before he would take vengeance on the cities, "I shall come down and see," and yet he knew all things. And that was for nothing else, sir, but to show men such as you are that you should not carry out punishments unless you have prior knowledge that they are appropriate. And, sir, you have done quite the contrary to me today, for, sir, you have caused me much shame for something I am not guilty of. I pray God forgive you it." (Chap. 48, Windeatt, p. 153)

The mention of the "Holy Writte" ("Holy Writ") and of the "veniawnce on þe cyteys" ("vengeance on the cities") might indeed be a reference to Sodom and Gomorrah, as Carolyn Dinshaw has remarked in her challenging study of *The Book of Margery Kempe*.

The scholar, working in the field of Queer Studies, observes that the whole of this episode of confrontation with the Mayor of Leicester might be read with a focus on the concept of *queer*. Dinshaw remarks that Margery wears the white robe, "we perceive," because "she is a creature whose body does not fit her desires", so that "we perceive a queer"[97]. The paradox constituted by her wearing the white robe even though she is a wife and a mother is, according to Dinshaw, a result of the "perversion within the normative". In fact, she affirms that Margery's white clothes signal the "disjunction in an orthodox Christianity which establishes marriage as a sacrament yet always maintains its taint"[98]. Margery's *queerness* is therefore a challenge to her society and its norms, and in particular its "'Lawful' heteronormative relations". Her cross-dressing as a virgin, according to Dinshaw, signals a challenge to normative identitary categories such as those of the virgin, the wife, and the mother, when Margery, wife and mother of fourteen children, strives to preserve her image of (recovered) virginity, as authorized by the revelations and visions of her celestial bridegroom.

Margery shows a certain awareness that her assertion of chastity and her wearing of white clothes, are seen as a subversion of the social demands placed on women and that most of the accusations

---

97 C. Dinshaw, "Margery Kempe Writes Back", p. 149. On antinormative identities see S. Antosa, "Queer Sexualities, Queer Spaces: Antinormative Negotiations of Sexual Identities, Spaces and Places", in Ambrosini R., D. Corona and A. Contenti (eds), *Challenges for the 21ˢᵗ Century* (Cultural Workshop), 2011 (forthcoming).

98 *Ibidem*. On Margery's display of virginity see also S. Salih, "Like A Virgin? *The Book of Margery Kempe*", in *Versions of Virginity in Late Medieval England* (Cambridge: D. S. Brewer, 2001), pp. 166-241.

against her are based on her behaviour, her external acts of piety rather than her allegations of divine communing, as this passage shows:

> Than þe Meyr seyde to hit, "I wil wetyn why þow gost in white clothys, for I trowe þow art comyn hedyr to han a-wey owr wyuys fro us & ledyn hem wyth þe." "Syr," sche seyth, "ȝe xal not wetyn of my mowth why I go in white clothys; ȝe arn not worthy to wetyn it. But, ser, I wil tellyn it to þes worthy clerkys wyth good wil be þe maner of confessyon. Avyse hem ȝyf þei wyl telle it ȝow." (Capitulum 48, Meech and Allen, p. 116)
>
> Then the Mayor said to her, "I want to know why you go about in white clothes, for I believe you have come here to lure away our wives from us, and lead them off with you."
> "Sir," she said, "you shall not know from my mouth why I go about in white clothes; you are not worthy to know it. But, sir, I will gladly tell it to these worthy clerks by way of confession. Let them consider whether they will tell it to you." (Chap. 48, Windeatt, p. 153)

By focusing on her white robes and on the ring her prosecutors show that the real danger represented by Margery lies in a woman preacher travelling around England (and across the world), and leading astray other women, thus disrupting the social order. Dinshaw goes further on this point, proposing a reading focused on the play of counteraccusations in which she suggests, by means of textual and contextual elements that the mayor and Margery might be exchanging reciprocal allegations of sodomy; according to Dinshaw, Margery or her amanuensis did not dare name this explicitly[99].

When she is detained in Leicester, she seems to be suggesting to the readers that she has been accused by a man to whom she has been rude. The significance of the meeting with this man might seem initially to have no meaning at that point of the narrative. However, Margery might be suggesting that she was imprisoned

---

99   See C. Dinshaw, "Margery Kempe Writes Back", p. 155.

by the mayor of Leicester simply because of the people's malice and ill-will towards her appearance and behaviour:

> Whan it was ouyr-comyn, sche goyng owt at þe chirche dore, a man toke hit be þe sleue & seyd, "Damsel, why wepist þu so sor?" "Ser," sche seyd, "it is not ʒow to telle." [...] þe osteler cam vp to hir chawmbyr in gret hast & toke a-wey hir scryppe & bad hyr comyn ʒerne and spekyn wyth þe Meyr. & so sche dede. Þan þe Meyr askyd hir of what cuntre sche was & whos dowtyr sche was. "Syr," sche seyd, "I am of Lynne in Norfolke, a good mannys dowtyr of þe same Lynne, whech hath ben meyr fyve tymes of þat worshepful burwgh and aldyrman also many ʒerys, & I haue a good man, also a burgeys of þe seyd town, Lynne, to myn husbond." "A," seyd þe Meyr, "Seynt Kateryn telde what kynred sche cam of & ʒet ar ʒe not lyche, for þu art a fals strumpet, a fals loller, & a fals deceyuer of þe pepyl, & þerfor I xal haue þe in preson." (Capitulum 48, Meech and Allen, pp. 111-112)

> When it [a fit of crying] was overcome, she going out at the church door, a man took her by the sleeve and said, "Damsel, why weep you so sorely?" "Sir," she said, "it is not meant to tell you." [...]
> The hosteler came up to her chamber in great haste and took away her scrip and bade her come quickly and speak with the mayor. And so she did.
> Then the mayor asked her of what country she was and whose daughter she was.
> "Sir," she said, "I am of Lynn in Norfolk, a good man's daughter of the same Lynn, who has been mayor five times of that worshipful town and alderman also many years, and I have a good man, also a burgess of the said town, Lynn, for my husband."
> "A," said the mayor, "Saint Katherine told what kindred she came of and yet you are not like her, for you are a false strumpet, a false Lollard, and a false deceiver of the people, and therefore I shall have you in prison." (Chap. 48, Windeatt, pp. 153)

What emerges from Margery's trials is her strength in subverting social roles. Accused of being a Lollard, she answers correctly to all the articles of faith, but her trials continue on the social level. Margery is a threat to social order because most of her actions go against the accepted functions of women in society and she is overtly reproached because she does not adhere to female roles:

> So, as sche went forth to-Beuerloward w*yth*þe seyd ȝemen & þe frerys be-forn-seyd, þei mettyn many tymes w*yth* men of þe cu*n*tre, whech seyd vn-to hir, "Damsel, forsake þis lyfe þat þu hast, & go spynne & carde as oþer women don, & suffyr not so meche schame & so meche wo [...]". (Capitulum 53, Meech and Allen, p. 129)

> So, as she went on toward Beverley with the said yeomen and friars, they many times met with men of that district, who said to her, "Woman, give up this life that you lead, and go and spin, and card wool, as other women do, and do not suffer so much shame and so much unhappiness". (95-6)

The rebuke from the men who meet Margery on her travels is grounded in fear of what such unconventional behaviour might foment in their ordinary (and normative) lives and relations. It is interesting to observe how in the mercantile area where Margery lived, on the east coast of England, women's social functions are seen in terms of commodification, and apart from mothers and wives they are considered as producers: "go spynne & carde as oþer women don" ("go and spin, and card wool, as other women do").

Subverting the process of abjection

Judith Butler draws on the theory of abjection expounded by Julia Kristeva in *Powers of Horror*, remarking how the body constitutes the boundary between the internal and external dimensions of the subject. The subject, she believes, perceives the Other, the "not-me", through the differences, through the elements of identity which have been rejected, thus isolating the Other as the abject:

> The boundary of the body as well as the distinction between internal and external is established through the ejection and transvaluation of something originally part of identity into a defiling otherness[100].

According to her the internal and the external cannot be considered as two distinct "realities", because they finally come into contact with each other, "becoming other"; this provocative hypothesis might be useful, as we shall see, in illustrating the last point in our reading of *The Book of Margery Kempe,* that of abjection:

> The boundary between inner and outer is confounded by those excremental passages in which the inner effectively becomes outer, and this excreting function becomes, as it were, the model by which other forms of identity-differentiation are accomplished. In effect, this is the mode by which Others become shit. For inner and outer worlds to remain utterly distinct, the entire surface of the body would have to achieve an impossible impermeability. This sealing of its surfaces would constitute the seamless boundary of the subject; but this enclosure would invariably be exploded by precisely that excremental filth that it fears[101].

This passage about Butler's conceptualization of abjection allows us to analyse, in the same light, some of the episodes in which Margery Kempe mentions the excreting bodily functions, whilst at the same time distancing herself from them. Could Margery not have spotlighted those moments when she was scornfully rejected as abject by other pilgrims, citizens and clergy, by describing their "vilest" bodily functions?

Actually, the acts of "voiding unclean matter", both defecating and vomiting, occur many times in her narrative and seem to follow those moments in which Margery has been publicly rejected, namely when she is repeatedly deserted by the "worshipful woman of London" during her journey back to England from Germany (in the second book, chapter 8), and when she is interro-

---

100 J. Butler, *Gender Trouble*, p. 170.
101 *Ibidem.*

gated by the Archbishop of York because she had been accused by a doctor of divinity and others of being a Lollard and a wicked woman.

As we are often reminded, Margery is not like other women. She does not respect the demands that Christian society places on women and for this reason she is rejected as abject. Moreover, as we have seen, her enactment of virginity overtly clashes with her motherhood; besides, Margery is not even a widow, like other female saints who are mentioned in the *Book*[102]. Indeed, she has asked her husband to make a vow of chastity and has left his house to assure everybody of their abstention from sexual intercourse. She defends herself from the allegations of wickedness by saying that she has already given him fourteen children, thus fulfilling her duty as mother and "breeder". Furthermore, as mentioned above, she has asked for permission to wear white, publicly proclaiming the purity which God has vouchsafed her.

In the first case, Margery helps the "worshipful woman of London" and those from her household who are suffering from seasickness on their voyage back to England from Calais. Before boarding the ship, the company had been continually fleeing from Margery, who, nonetheless, desperate for fellowship, continues stalking them. In the end, after a sudden and inexplicable change of ship (Margery remarks that "what the cause was she knew never"), she manages to board their same ship, and is, once more, greeted by hostility:

> Þe seyd creatur, parceyuyng þorw her cher & cuntenawnce þat þei had lityl affeccyon to hit persone, preyid to owr Lord þat he wolde grawntyn hir grace to holdyn hir heuyd up & preseruyn hir fro voidyng of vnclene mater

---

102 On Margery performances of virginity, see S. Salih, "Like A Virgin? *The Book of Margery Kempe*", and also L. McAvoy, "Virgin, Mother, Whore: The Sexual Spirituality of Margery Kempe", in Chewning S. M. (ed.) *Intersections of Sexuality and the Divine in Medieval Culture: The Word Made Flesh* (Aldershot: Ashgate, 2005), pp. 121-138.

> in her *p*resens, so þ*at* sche schulde cawsyn hem non abhominacyon. (Capitulum 8, Book 2, Meech and Allen, p. 242)

> The said creature, perceiving from their faces and expressions that they had little affection for her, prayed to our Lord that he would grant her grace to hold her head up, and preserve her from bringing up vomit in their presence, so that she should cause them no abhorrence. (Chap. 8, Book 2, Windeatt, pp. 286-287)

Margery is continually rejected by her travelling companions, mainly because of her excesses in the physical manifestations of her devotion and contrition, which are expressed through bodily phenomena (such as weeping and swooning); now however, saved by God's (requested) intervention, it is she who witnesses the bodily excess of seasickness:

> Hir desyr was fulfillyd so þ*at*, oþ*er* in þe schip voydyng & castyng ful boistowsly & vnclenly, sche, her alderys m*er*uelyng, myth helpyn hem & do what sche wolde. And specialy þe woman of London had most of þ*at* passyon & þ*at* infirmite, to whom þis creatur was most besy to helpyn & c*om*fortyn for owr Lord*ys* loue & be charite, – oþ*er* cawse had sche non. (Capitulum 8, Book 2, Meech and Allen, p. 242)

> Her desire was fulfilled, so that, while others in the ship were throwing up very violently and foully, she was able – to the amazement of them all – to help them and do what she wished. And the woman from London especially had the worst of that sickness, and this creature was most busy to help her and comfort her for our Lord's love and charity – she had no other reason. (Chap. 8, Book 2, Windeatt, pp. 286-287)

Here the tone of her narrative turns out to be comical and "humbly" triumphant. Margery had been excluded from the company and the worshipful woman had forcefully rejected her, saying:

> "What wenyst þu for to gon w*yth* me? Nay, I do þe wel to wetyn I wyl not medelyn w*yth* þe." (Capitulum 8, Book 2, Meech and Allen, p. 240)

> "What! do you think to go with me? No, I'll have you know that I'll not get involved with you" (Chap. 8, Book 2, Windeatt, p. 284).

The term "medelyn" ("get involved", meddle) brings to mind the mixing of different material substances or fluids; Margery is pointed out as unclean and unworthy, but the narrative introduces a reversal of the condition of abjection. The situation is subverted and the uncleanness that the worshipful woman had seen in Margery is now literally expelled by the woman herself. She is thus compelled to meddle with the same Margery who, whilst holding her head up ("holdyn hir heuyd up"), helps her in the name of God: "for owr Lordys loue & be charite, – oþer cawse had sche non" ("for our Lord's love and charity – she had no other reason"). Thus, the worshipful woman and the unworthy creature manifestly come into physical contact, temporarily reconciled by the much-detested filth.

In the tale of the priest and the bear which Margery recounts to the Archbishop of York, we find many of the terms we have met before, all linked to the semantic field of abjection: "abomination", "void", "uncleanness". These relate to the displacement of the boundary between the inner and outer. In the tale the inner uncleanliness of the priest, who soils the sacrament of ministry, becomes manifest in the actions, or rather, *exemplum*, performed by the bear:

> "Sir, wyth ȝowr reuerens, I spak but of o preste be þe maner of exampyl, þe whech as I haue lernyd went wil in a wode thorw pe sufferawns of God for þe profite of hys sowle tyl þe nygth cam up-on hym. He, destytute of hys herborwe, fond a fayr erber in þe whech he restyd þat nyght, hauyng a fayr pertre in þe myddys al floreschyd wyth flowerys & belschyd, and blomys ful delectabil to hys syght, wher cam a bere, gret & boistows, hogely to beheldyn, schakyng &e pertre & fellyng down þe flowerys. Gredily þis greuows best ete & deuowryd þo fayr flowerys. &, whan he had etyn hem, turnyng hys tayl-ende in pe prestys presens, voydyd hem owt ageyn at þe hymyr party." (Capitulum 52, Meech and Allen, p. 127)

> "Sir, by your reverence, I only spoke of one priest, by way of example, who, as I have learned it, went astray in a wood – through the sufferance of God, for the profit of his soul – until night came upon him. Lacking any shelter, he found a

73

> fair arbour in which he rested that night, which had a beautiful pear-tree in the middle, all covered in blossoms, which he delighted to look at. To that place came a great rough bear, ugly to behold, that shook the pear-tree and caused the blossoms to fall. Greedily this horrible beast ate and devoured those fair flowers. And, when he had eaten them, turning his tail towards the priest, he discharged them out again at his rear end." (Chap. 52, Windeatt, pp. 165-166)

Margery here takes on the role of preacher and lays the charge of depravity on some of the representatives of the clergy who are accusing her. At the same time, through her counter-accusation, which is expressed perfectly in the style of a sermon through the use of the *exemplum*, she is building up an image of herself as a holy woman in opposition to the priest who has accused her of being wicked and who, on the contrary, himself proves to be corrupt.

> "Þe preste, hauyng gret abhominacyon of þat lothly syght, conceyuyng gret heuynes dowte what it myth mene, on þe next day he wandrid forth in hys wey al heuy & pensife, whom it fortunyd to metyn wyth a semly agydd man lych to a palmyr era pilgrime, þe whiche enqwiryd of þe preste þe cawse of hys heuynes. The preste, rehersyng þe mater be-forn-wretyn, seyd he conceyuyd gret drede & heuynes whan he beheld þat lothly best defowlyn & deuowryn so fayr flowerys & blomys & aftirward so horrybely to deuoydyn hem be-for hym at hys tayl-ende, & he not vndirstondyng what þis myth mene". (Capitulum 52, Meech and Allen, p. 127)

> "The priest, greatly revolted at that disgusting sight and becoming very depressed for fear of what it might mean, wandered off on his way all gloomy and pensive. He happened to meet a good-looking, aged man like a pilgrim, who asked the priest the reason for his sadness. The priest, repeating the matter written before, said he felt great fear and heaviness of heart when he beheld that revolting beast soil and devour such lovely flowers and blossoms, and afterwards discharge them so horribly at his rear end in the priest presence – he did not understand what this might mean." (Chap. 52, Windeatt, pp. 165-166)

It is highly significant that the bodily language which has so far characterised the mystical experience and the visions of Christ in this *exemplum* now takes on a completely different twist. The narrative respects all the formal characteristics of the *exempla*, which also feature the presence of a messenger of God giving a warning to unruly Christians before punishing them. This element was called to mind in Margery's mention of the biblical episode of Sodom and Gomorrah.

There are no more vestiges of the language of marital love, where physicality is far removed from the carnal uncleanness often attributed to sexual relations, even within marriage (the "taint" Dinshaw refers to). The language used here might more readily exemplify the unworded accusation that the Mayor of Leicester moved to Margery. The pear-tree, a symbol of purity, is fouled by the bear's actions, explicitly representing bestiality.

> "Than þe palmyr, schewyng hym-selfe þe massanger of God, þus aresond hym, 'Preste, þu þi-self art pe pertre, sumdel florischyng & floweryng thorw þi Seruyse seyyng & þe Sacramentys ministryng, thow þu do vndeuowtly, for þu takyst ful lytyl heede how þu seyst þi Mateynes & þi Seruyse, so it be blaberyd to an ende. Þan gost þu to þi Messe wyth-owtyn deuocyon, & for þi synne hast þu ful lityl contricyon. Þu receyuyst þerþe frute of euyr-lestyng lyfe, þe Sacrament of þe Awter, in ful febyl disposicyon. Sithyn al þe day aftyr þu myssespendist þi tyme, þu ʒeuist þe to byyng & sellyng, choppyng & chongyng, as it wer a man of þe werld. Þu sittyst at þe | ale, ʒeuyng þe to glotonye & excesse, to lust of thy body, thorw letchery & vnclennesse. Þu brekyst þe comawndmentys of God thorw sweryng, lying, detraccyon, & bakbytyng, & swech oþer synnes vsyng. Thus be thy mysgouernawns, lych on-to þe lothly ber, þu deuowryst & destroist &e flowerys & blomys of vertuows leuyng to thyn endles dampnacyon & many mannys hyndryng lesse þan þu haue grace of repentawns & amendyng." (Capitulum 52, Meech and Allen, p. 127)

> "Then, the pilgrim, showing himself to be the messenger of God, thus addressed him, 'Priest, you are yourself the pear-tree, somewhat flourishing and flowering through your saying of services and administering of sacraments, although you act without devotion, for you take very little heed how you say your matins and your service, so long as it is babbled to an end. Then you go to your mass without devotion, and you have very little contrition for your sin. You receive there the fruit of everlasting life, the sacrament of the altar, in a very feeble frame of mind. All day long afterwards,

you spend your time amiss: you give yourself over to buying and selling, bartering and exchanging, just like a man of the world. You sit over your beer, giving yourself up to gluttony and excess, to the lust of your body, through lechery and impurity. You break the commandments of God through swearing, lying, detraction and backbiting gossip, and the practice of other such sins. Thus, through your misconduct, just like the loathsome bear, you devour and destroy the flowers and blossoms of virtuous living, to your own endless damnation and to the hindrance of many other people, unless you have grace from repentance and amending." (Chap. 52, Windeatt, pp. 165-166)

In this case the language of filth overtly refers to the realm of sin, with an emphasis on expressions such as "glotonye", "lust of thy body", "letchery" and "vnclennesse" (gluttony, lust, lechery, impurity), which explicitly make reference to the domain of Christian law: the Commandments.

Margery's victory is emphasised by the priest himself eventually confessing that the tale bitterly upsets him ("[...] þis tale smytyth me to þe hert", Capitulum 52, Meech and Allen, p. 127; "[...] this tale smites me to the heart", Chap. 52, Windeatt, p. 166).

CHAPTER 4

A Contemporary Re-Writing: Eva Figes's *The True Tale of Margery Kempe*

In 1985, BBC Radio 2 broadcast a radio play by contemporary Anglo-German writer Eva Figes (1932): *The True Tale of Margery Kempe*. The text, so far unpublished in book form, is quite compelling since, at first glance, it might appear to be a mere dramatization of *The Book of Margery Kempe*[103]. However, we feel that the narrative strategies adopted by Eva Figes in this adaptation for radio of the medieval text are informed by the hypotheses that Figes must have made on the creation of *The Book of Margery Kempe* and in particular on the authorial voice.

Figes's adaptation of the text leaves most of the words in the original manuscript unaltered. The transformation of the medium from written text to oral text, however, gives her the opportunity, through directions to the actors, to underline the role of Margery as narrator and author of the work. This position is not surprising for a writer who has been committed to the feminist struggle since the early 1960s, devoting her writing, both fiction and non-fiction, to the history and rights of women[104].

---

103 We make reference to a copy of the script of *The True Tale of Margery Kempe*, dramatized by Eva Figes (1985), obtained from BBC Radio in 2005.
104 Her *Patriarchal Attitudes. Women in Society* (London: Virago, 1970) and *Sex and Subterfuge: Women Writers to 1850* (Basingstoke: Palgrave Macmillan, 1982) are remembered as two milestones among feminist classics. On her memoir *Little Eden: A Child at War* (London: Faber, 1978) see D. Corona, "Al di qua del paradiso. Memoria spaziale e confini del rifugio in

When she wrote *The True Tale of Margery Kempe,* Eva Figes had already written other radio plays for BBC Radio and was therefore well aware of the tools at her command. Among her radio plays written prior to 1985, we might mention *Time Regained* (1980), *Dialogue Between Friends* (1982), and *Punch-flame and Pigeon-Breast* (1983).

It is interesting to note that this adaptation to the oral medium is quite appropriate, since *The Book of Margery Kempe* was dictated to scribes and also because the text makes use of a form of dramatic representation which was borrowed from contemporary miracle plays; Margery often dwelled at length on her visions of the Nativity scenes, Christ and the Virgin Mary, the Passion of Christ, as well as his resurrection.

Another aspect we shall be taking into consideration is the way in which Figes deals with Margery's sexuality and with her ostentation of virginity. We shall see whether the issue of Margery's active sexual life and her desire to be seen in public as a virgin is challenged in this version for contemporary readers.

Back to orality

In conversation with Olga Kenyon, with regard to her novels, Eva Figes once affirmed that form is really important to her writing because "it gives you a structure"[105]. We might well argue that form is the most important element in *The True Tale of Margery*

Little Eden. A Child at War di Eva Figes", in Chialant M. T. and Bottalico M. (eds), *L'impulso autobiografico* (Napoli: Liguori, 2005), pp. 45-61.
105 O. Kenyon, "Eva Figes", in *Women Writers Talk. Interviews with Ten Women Writers* (London: Lennard Publishing, 1989), p. 80.

Kempe, although this might seem obvious since we are talking about a radio play.

First of all, radio plays are usually rather short, so this genre is dependent on limitations of time. It takes less than fifty minutes to perform the play, which is exactly right for a radio programme. Since the work is meant to be read out aloud, the enunciation of the sentences is rather simple and clear and is arranged in dialogues and monologues, often followed by a chorus and other voices which keep changing as the scene changes.

The radio play covers more than half of the first book of *The Book of Margery Kempe*, including the main episodes and themes here presented through the voice of Margery and through dialogues with other figures from the text of origin. The episodes referred to cover her conversion, her first visions of Christ and her pilgrimages around England and abroad. The events recounted in the play focus on the encounters with the Mayor of Leicester and stop somewhat abruptly with the proposed visit to the Archbishop of York (something which is merely hinted at). However, Figes chose to close the play with the final words in chapter 89, which is the last chapter in Book 1.

It is interesting to observe how Figes entrusts the narration of the events merely to one voice, that of Margery, whilst giving her two personae: her monologues are in the third person addressed to an invisible audience, whereas the first person is used in dialogues with her husband and Christ, suggesting intimacy between the characters. Sometimes the third person and the first person are inter-changed in the same line, thus creating a vocal representation of the sudden mystic rapture. The mystical embrace and intimate dalliance with Jesus (as Figes calls him, thus emphasising his manhood) are further emphasised and introduced through the use of music presented in the script through the author's directions. There are musical interludes in the play whenever Jesus enters the dialogue or in preparation for his entry, as for instance when Margery enters a church to seek spiritual counsel.

This continuous shift from the third to the first person – both characteristic of autobiographical writing – also signals a distancing of Margery the narrator from the narrated persona, especially when she describes the sinful life of her youth and when she talks about her material and sexual temptations (all episodes from the original text). As Smith and Watson have pointed out:

> When we read autobiographical texts, they often seem to be 'speaking' to us. We 'hear' a narrative voice distinctive in its emphasis and tone, its rhythms and syntax, its lexicon and affect. But theorizing voice as a construct in life writing has not yet been the focus of sustained critical attention[106].

What has not been done yet on the critical level is here achieved on a creative level. Figes works on some of the formal features of autobiography – narrator, narratee, and orality – mixing them with those of the radio play and at the same time providing a creative response for those conflicts emerging from a contemporary reading of *The Book of Margery Kempe*. This alternation of the third and first person might in fact raise the issue of the presence of the scribe in the *Book* and of the influence it might have had on Margery's life story as dictated to a scribe. Figes excludes from the very start the presence of the scribes by entrusting the first lines of the play to the direct voice of the woman (preceded by her name and a column, "Margery:", as is normally done in dialogues). Besides, the writer does not mention the episode concerning the origins of the *Book*, which were on the contrary clearly described in the Proem in the text of origin.

The radio play thus gives back to *The Book of Margery Kempe* its oral nature of a life dictated to a scribe, making use of

---

[106] S. Smith and J. Watson, *Reading Autobiography*, p. 79.

reconstructed dialogues and interior monologues, which bring to mind the composition of collaborative life writing[107].

Sexuality and virginity

One of the most surprising and innovative aspects in Eva Figes's radio play is her inclusion of explicit references to Margery's sexual life, her temptations and her pleasure. *The Book of Margery Kempe* clearly described Margery's conflict between her married life and her desire to validate her public figure through the ostentation of her purity, acknowledged by the heavenly marriage to Christ.

In *The True Tale of Margery Kempe* Figes includes "sounds of love-making", thus stressing Margery's pleasure in her sexual encounters with her husband. These descriptions might be somewhat disturbing for the contemporary audience but they are the direct consequence of a modernization strategy in which the author attempts to restore to her character those everyday elements excluded from the narrative in the original text, possibly because of its devotional quality and the presence of the first listeners, the two scribes[108].

Desire is presented from the very first lines as the propelling force of the narration. It is not only sexual desire which is at the centre of this play, Figes underlines Margery's desire for self-

---

107 For useful notes and references on collaborative life writing and oral life narrative see S. Smith and J. Watson, *Reading Autobiography*, in particular, respectively, pp. 66, 79.
108 These destabilizing elements of carnality are taken further in Robert Glück's novel, as mentioned above, creating a fictional interpretation of Margery's *queerness* as a breach of normative behaviours. For an analysis of Glück's *Margery Kempe*, see the last part of C. Dinshaw, "Margery Kempe Writes Back", pp. 164-173.

affirmation. This theme opens the narration as Margery recounts the immediate crisis of her marriage and the birth of her first child and, distancing herself from the narrated persona, she describes her desire to establish her social status through her own business activities. The voices of the chorus, representing those who worked with her, receive this anomalous desire, as something arising out of evil and witchcraft. Figes identifies Margery with witches, which is a way of reiterating that heretics and witches shared the same fate. In the *Book*, Margery risks being burnt at the stake more than once following the charge of Lollardy. The voice of the common people thus moves Margery's *queerness* into the field of popular culture, where witches are feared more than heretics.

Uncontrolled female sexual desire was demonized in medieval culture (both religious and popular) and Figes lays the stress on this aspect in a dialogue between Margery and her husband, which is more overt and explicit than in the *Book*. John (who is actually identified merely as "husband" and has no name in the play) keeps tickling Margery whilst she starts talking about the glory of heavens. Margery, whose conversations with her confessor are recorded as happening before she had had any visions of Jesus, observes that it would be better for them to live in chastity, abandoning the mutual pleasures they share.

Figes's radio play questions the relationship between Margery and her confessors by showing that her quest for chastity and her ostentation of "performed" virginity might be the result of the severe rebukes from her spiritual fathers.

The previously-mentioned "sounds of love-making" are included in a monologue in which Margery affirms that she would rather "drink the ooze and muck of the gutter" than allow her husband to enter into carnal union. Of course, the "gasps" and "grunts" which regularly interrupt her monologue betray quite different feelings, which she justifies as obedience to her husband[109].

109 E. Figes, *The True Tale of Margery Kempe*, p. 5.

Figes's contemporary re-reading/rewriting of *The Book of Margery Kempe* and the actual figure of Margery thus anticipate the critical approach of scholars studying the *Book* between the end of the 20th and the beginning of the 21st centuries. Her radio play leaves us suspended creatively between the medieval readers and the contemporary audience, restoring to the book and Margery the prominence they merit in the history of literature.

Conclusions

The most recent re-readings and rewritings of *The Book of Margery Kempe* bring to light the multiple levels of interpretation that a text dating back to the 15th century provides today.

The intriguing relationship between the physical and the spiritual is drawing ever greater attention from scholars working in the fields of Women's Studies, Gender Studies and, more recently, Queer Studies. Contemporary criticism is increasingly interested in examining the identity conflicts which emerge from the impossibility of conforming totally to social expectations of normativity. Furthermore, ancient texts such as *The Book of Margery Kempe* enable contemporary writers to create in their rewriting a representation of subjects – drawing on key-figures such as Margery Kempe – who subvert dominant discourses. Both critical re-readings and creative rewritings of Margery Kempe's character and text, as we have seen, question the field of conflict by contemplating some of the aspects of the narrative which had not been taken into consideration until the 1990s. The ulterior development of Women's Studies in the 1980s enabled scholars active in this field to give fresh interpretations to this text as autobiography, opening up the way to the more recent positions, which take as their starting points concepts such as *performance* and *queerness*.

A contemporary reading of a medieval text as multilayered as *The Book of Margery Kempe,* also raises the issue of the current perception of spirituality and sexuality in relation to subjects whose identity boundaries are now seen as mobile and beyond traditional definitions of fixity. Today, the text itself is enjoying a new lease of life, something which has been made possible following the revision of the literary canon triggered by Women's Studies and Cultural Studies.

In our analysis of *The Book of Margery Kempe* and the figure of Margery Kempe herself, we have focused on the themes of gender and sexuality in the representation of the public roles attained by Margery Kempe as mystic, (outlaw) preacher and pilgrim.

The first analyses of the *Book*, in fact, focused merely on Margery's mysticism, often accusing her of hysteria because of her unconventionality. Compared with her contemporary anchoress Julian of Norwich, a canonical mystic-theologian, Margery appeared to be rather an eccentric mystic.

Acknowledged as the first autobiography in English, and written in the vernacular, it has attracted many works dealing with the question of literary authority. The presence of the scribes raises questions about the influence these might have had on her narrative, although, as we have seen, contemporary literary criticism often finds in Margery a clear authorial voice able to make use of precise narrative strategies. It is Margery's comments on the role of women in society and her confrontations with religious and political authorities in particular that suggest that Margery has authorial independence. She is aware of the idea of authority, which she sees mirrored in the external Authority of God legitimating her text, travels, and public-speaking.

The focus on the concept of authorship has at its basis the idea that Margery is not as illiterate as she claims to be. On the contrary, she seems to be aware of the narrative conventions of literary genres like hagiography and of those used by women mystics. Contemporary criticism has reconsidered the relationship between women and learning, showing that in medieval society it was not necessary to read in order to cultivate oneself, since "public orality" and "community of discourse" were the main means of learning.

Her description of herself as an illiterate woman is another instrument of legitimation, since it also justifies the presence of the male scribe. This then authorizes the writing and the circulation of a book about the life of a married woman claiming to be visited by God. The text, in fact, includes elements belonging to different literary forms which could all be included in self-referential writing: autobiography, hagiography, spiritual life writing, oral life-story, and travel narrative.

The new critical perspectives on Margery's life-narrative link the narration of her spiritual development with the description of her material preoccupations.

From this point of view, the account of her pilgrimages includes many comments regarding the material conditions which Margery had to endure on her travels and the encounters she had on her way to the holy shrines and back home again.

The Book of Margery Kempe is considered an important historical document illustrating, from a critical perspective, the social context of Christian England between the 14th and the 15th centuries, with a specific focus on the representatives of the Church and on civil authorities.

The Book has also recently been receiving increasing attention from scholars working within the field of travel writing, since it is one of the few surviving medieval travel accounts written in the vernacular by a female pilgrim, although at the time quite a number of women did go on pilgrimages.

Margery's pilgrimages have a prominent role in the description of her self-empowerment because the spiritual transformation she undergoes during her travels eventually gives her the right to speak in public. Her loquacity increases proportionately every time she comes back from one of her spiritual journeys. This is explained by the nature of the pilgrimage. In fact, visiting the places where Jesus Christ or a saint had lived enabled pilgrims to live their lives in imitation of them, which would contribute to their spiritual growth. As a matter of fact, Margery is seen to have been completely transformed following her pilgrimage to the Holy Land. In Italy, Margery behaves like a Samaritan, devoting herself to the care of the needy.

Thus, the representation of Margery's identity works on different levels: as a mystic, as a preacher, and as a pilgrim.

However, her identity as a holy woman is menaced by her unconventional behaviour, her spiritual self always being indissolubly linked to her bodiliness. Her visions, her acts of contrition (copious during her pilgrimages) and her language are deeply-rooted in corporeal images, which often hint at a sexual context. As we have seen, McAvoy argues that Margery is able to negotiate the representation of her identity as a woman through her sexualized body crossing all boundaries.

Dinshaw maintains that through the performative enactment of the role of the virgin, Margery was able to question the normativity of the social functions of women. She thus attains a social position from which to make her voice heard, whilst recovering agency in her representation of herself.

Margery Kempe plays with gender stereotypes based on female sexuality and acts them out with the aim of legitimizing her speaking voice. However, the conflict between the medieval conception of women's bodies as providers for the family's procreation, on the one hand, and that of the demonization of their carnality, on the other, leads to an identity conflict which is recorded on her body and is expressed by her insistence on the preservation of her image of virginity.

As we have seen, Carolyn Dinshaw's innovative reading of *The Book of Margery Kempe* questions Margery's performances of virginity. The paradox of a mother of fourteen children striving with all her strength to appear to be a virgin hints at a discomfort with the normative roles of femininity, all of which makes Margery out to be a *queer*.

Margery's anti-normative behaviour defies social institutions such as marriage in which women were always subordinated to their husbands. Although these modern ideas could not be uttered in a medieval text, there emerges in the words of Margery an awareness of her ability to disrupt social norms, and in fact, she is accused of corrupting other women.

Thus, *The Book of Margery Kempe* delineates a crossing of boundaries, in which speech and the body are the sites for the redefinition of Margery's identity. Margery's figure can be read in terms of *queerness* because of her continuous attempts at breaking social conventions through her actions and her words.

Her words often converge on bodily functions, implying the emission of bodily substances; this might arouse disgust in her listeners and her insisting on such details makes an abject figure of her.

It is challenging to read Margery's representation of the body from the perspective of the theory of abjection proposed by Julia Kristeva and further developed by Judith Butler. In language like Margery's where inconvenient images of the body crop up continually, the representation of the body directs attention towards the links between the internal and external aspects of the subject always viewed in its relationship with the Other (different from the self). What lies beyond the self is rejected as abject, and considered as corrupting Otherness.

Eva Figes's rewriting of *The Book of Margery Kempe* in her radio play *The True Tale of Margery* Kempe, broadcast in 1985, anticipates most of the themes which were later to be developed by literary critics.

Her narrative techniques point to issues regarding literary authority and the oral quality of *The Book of Margery Kempe,* further emphasised by Figes's decision to use the term "tale" in her title. Singling out some of the formal characteristics of the original text, Figes offers a creative re-reading/re-writing of the *Book* which creates links between Margery Kempe and the contemporary readers.

The writer's insistence on Margery's sexuality (and sexual activity in the first pages of the script) is an anticipation of the critical interpretations flourishing since the 1990s.

The choice of the genre of a radio play for an adaptation of this medieval book is a further confirmation of the common direction shared by contemporary interpreters of *The Book of Margery Kempe*. Those writers and critics who make of *performance* the key-concept for the interpretation of *The Book of Margery Kempe* show how this text keeps assuming fresh multiple meanings, many of which are still to be investigated.

References

Cited Works

Aers D., *Community, Gender and Individual Identity. English Writing 1360-1430* (London: Routledge, 1988).

Antosa S., "Queer Sexualities, Queer Spaces: Antinormative Negotiations of Sexual Identities, Spaces and Places", in Ambrosini R., D. Corona and A. Contenti (eds), *Challenges for the 21st Century* (Cultural Workshop), 2011 (forthcoming).

Ashley K., "Historicizing Margery: The Book of Margery Kempe as Social Text", *The Journal of Medieval and Early Modern Studies*, 28, 2 (1998), pp. 371-389.

Ballard G., "Memoirs of Margery Kempe", in *Memoirs of Several Ladies of Great Britain: Who Have Been Celebrated for Their Writings or Skill in the Learned Languages Arts and Sciences* (Oxford: Printed by W. Jackson for the author, 1752), p. 8.

Barratt A. (ed.), *Women's Writings in Middle English* (London and New York: Longman, 1992).

Beckwith S., "A Very Material Mysticism: The Medieval Mysticism of Margery Kempe", in Aers D. (ed.), *Medieval Literature. Criticism, Ideology and History* (Brighton: Harvester Press, 1986), pp. 34-57.

Beckwith S., "Problems of Authority in Late Medieval English Mysticism: Language, Agency, and Authority in *The Book of Margery Kempe*", *Exemplaria*, 4, 1 (1992), pp. 171-199.

Bennett J., "Medievalism and Feminism", in Partner N. F. (ed.), *Studying Medieval Women. Sex, Gender, Feminism* (Cambridge, Massachussetts: The Medieval Academy of America, 1993), pp. 7-29.

Benstock S. (ed.), *The Private Self. The Theory and Practice of Women's Autobiographical Writings* (London & New York: Routledge, 1988).

Bolton Holloway J., Bechtold J. and Wright C., "Introduction: The Body and the Book", in Bolton Holloway J. et al. (eds), *Equally in God's Image: Women in the Middle Ages* (New York and Berne: Peter Lang), 1990, pp. 1-23.

Bolton Holloway J. et al. (eds), *Equally in God's Image: Women in the Middle Ages* (New York and Berne: Peter Lang), 1990.

Bradford C., "Mother, Maiden, Child: Gender as Performance in *The Book of Margery Kempe*", in Devlin-Glass F. and L. McCredden (eds) *Feminist Poetics of the Sacred: Creative Suspicions* (Oxford: Oxford University Press, 2001), pp. 165-181.

Butler J., *Gender Trouble* (London: Routledge, 1990).

Castagna V., "Margery Kempe and Her Becoming Authoress", *Textus* 19, 2 (2006), pp. 323-338.

Castagna V., "Margery Kempe: una mistica del quattrocento in pellegrinaggio", *Fogli di Anglistica* 1, 1-2 n.s. (2007), pp. 83-91.

Chialant M. T. and Bottalico M. (eds), *L'impulso autobiografico* (Napoli: Liguori, 2005).

Cholmeley K., *Margery Kempe. Genius and Mystic* (London: Green & Co., 1947).

Collis L., *Memoirs of a Medieval Woman: The Life and Times of Margery Kempe* (New York: Thomas Y. Crowell Company, 1964).

Corona D., "Al di qua del paradiso. Memoria spaziale e confini del rifugio in *Little Eden. A Child at War* di Eva Figes", in Chialant M. T. and Bottalico M. (eds), *L'impulso autobiografico* (Napoli: Liguori, 2005), pp. 45-61.

Cross R. C., "Oral Life, Written Text: The Genesis of *The Book of Margery Kempe*", *The Yearbook of English Studies* 22 (1992), pp. 226-237.

Cuddon J.A., *The Dictionary of Literary Terms & Literary Theory* (London: Penguin, 1999).

De Certeau M. [1980], "Mystic Speech", in *Heterologies. Discourse on the Other*, English trans. by B. Massumi (Manchester: Manchester University Press, 1986), pp. 80-100.

Delany S., "Sexual Economics", in Evans R. and L. Johnson (eds), *Feminist Readings in Middle English Literature. The Wife of Bath and All her Sect* (London and New York, Routledge: 1994), pp. 72-87.

Del Lungo Camiciotti G. (ed.), *Il libro di Margery Kempe. Autobiografia spirituale di una laica del Quattrocento* (Milano: Àncora, 2002).

Del Lungo Camiciotti G., "Il significato del digiuno nell'esperienza delle mistiche inglesi tardo medievali", *LC. Rivista Online del Dipartimento di Letterature e Culture Europee* II, 1 (2008), Università degli Studi di Palermo, <http://www.dilce.unipa.it/rivista/documenti/n_01_2008/09_g_dellungo.pdf>, last accessed December 2009, pp. 63-75.

Dinshaw C., "Margery Kempe Writes Back", in *Getting Medieval: Sexualities and Communities, Pre- and Postmodern* (Durham: Duke University Press, 1999), pp. 2143-182.

Douglas (1966), *Purity and Danger. An Analysis of Concept of Pollution and Taboo* (London and New York: Routledge, 2002).

Evans R. and L. Johnson (eds), *Feminist Readings in Middle English Literature. The Wife of Bath and All her Sect* (London and New York: Routledge, 1994).

Figes E., *Patriarchal Attitudes. Women in Society* (London: Virago, 1970).

Figes E., *Little Eden: A Child at War* (London: Faber, 1978).

Figes E., *Sex and Subterfuge: Women Writers to 1850* (Basingstoke: Palgrave Macmillan, 1982).

Figes E., *The True Tale of Margery Kempe* (London: BBC Radio 2, 1985).

Fortunati V. et al. (eds), *Studi di genere e memoria culturale. Women and Cultural Memory* (Bologna: CLUEB, 2004).

Furrow M., "Unscholarly Latinity and Margery Kempe", in Toswell M. J. and E. M. Tyler (eds), *Studies in English Language and Literature: Doubt Wisely, Papers in Honour of E. G. Stanley* (London: Routledge, 1996), pp. 240-251.

Gallyon M., *Margery Kempe of Lynn and Medieval England* (Norwich: The Canterbury Press, 1995).

Gibson McMurray G., "St. Margery: *The Book of Margery Kempe*", in Bolton Holloway J. et al. (eds), *Equally in God's Image: Women in the Middle Ages* (New York and Berne: Peter Lang, 1990), pp. 144-163.

Glenn C., "Author, Audience, and Autobiography: Rhetorical Technique in *The Book of Margery Kempe*", *College English* 54, 5 (1992), pp. 540-553.

Glenn C., "Reexamining *The Book of Margery Kempe:* A Rhetoric of Autobiography", in Lunsford A. (ed.), *Reclaiming Rhetorica: Women in the Rhetorical Tradition* (Pittsburgh: University of Pittsburgh Press, 1995), pp. 53-71.

Glück R., *Margery Kempe* (London: Serpent's Tail, 1994).

Goodman A., *Margery Kempe and Her World* (London & New York: Longman, 2002).

Harding W., "Body into Text: *The Book of Margery Kempe*", in Lomperis L. and S. Stanbury (eds), *Feminist Approaches to the Body in Medieval Literature* (Philadelphia: University of Pennsylvania Press, 1993), pp. 168-187.

Ho C., "Margery Reads Exempla", *Medieval Perspectives* (1993), pp. 143-152.

Hopenwasser N., "A Performance Artist and Her Performance Text: Margery Kempe on Tour", in Suydam M. A. and J. E. Ziegler (eds), *Performance and Transformation: New Approaches to Late Medieval Spirituality* (New York: St. Martin's Press, 1999), pp. 97-131.

Kenyon O., "Eva Figes", in *Women Writers Talk. Interviews with Ten Women Writers* (London: Lennard Publishing, 1989), pp. 71-90.

Knowles D., *The English Mystical Tradition* (London: Burns and Oates, 1961).

Kristeva J. (1980), *Powers of Horror. An Essay on Abjection*, English trans. by L. S. Roudiez (New York: Columbia University Press, 1982).

Locatelli C., "Is S/(he) My Gaze? (Feminist) Possibilities for Autobiographical Co(n)texts", in Chialant M. T. and Bottalico M. (eds), *L'impulso autobiografico* (Napoli: Liguori, 2005), pp. 3-18.

Long J., "Mysticism and Hysteria", in Evans R. and L. Johnson (eds), *Feminist Readings in Middle English Literature. The Wife of Bath and All her Sect* (London and New York: Routledge, 1994), pp. 88-111.

Lutrell A., "Englishwomen as Pilgrims to Jerusalem: Isolda Parewastell, 1365", in Bolton Holloway J. *et al.* (eds), *Equally in*

God's Image: Women and the Middle Ages (New York and Berne: Peter Lang), 1990, pp. 184-197.

McAvoy L., "Virgin, Mother, Whore: The Sexual Spirituality of Margery Kempe", in Chewning S. M. (ed.) *Intersections of Sexuality and the Divine in Medieval Culture: The Word Made Flesh* (Aldershot: Ashgate, 2005), pp. 121-138.

McAvoy L., "'[A]n Awngel Al Clothyd in White': Rereading the Book of Life as *The Book of Margery Kempe*", in Mulder-Bakker A. B. and L. McAvoy (eds), *Women and Experience in Later Medieval Writing: Reading the Book of Life* (New York: Palgrave Macmillan, 2009), pp. 103-122.

McCAnn J., "*The Book of Margery Kempe*", *Dublin Review*, 200 (1937), pp. 103-116.

Meech S. and H. E. Allen, *The Book of Margery Kempe* (London: Oxford University Press, 1940).

Minnis A., "Spiritualizing Marriage: Margery Kempe's Allegories of Female Authority", in *Translations of Authority in Medieval English Literature. Valuing the Vernacular* (Cambridge: Cambridge University Press, 2009), pp. 112-128.

Morrison S. S., *Women Pilgrims in Late Medieval England. Private Piety as Public Performance* (New York: Routledge, 2000).

Mulder-Bakker A. B. and L. McAvoy, "Experientia and the Construction of Experience in Medieval Writing: An Introduction", in Mulder-Bakker A. B. and L. McAvoy (eds), *Women and Experience in Later Medieval Writing: Reading the Book of Life* (New York: Palgrave Macmillan, 2009), pp. 1-23.

Mueller J. M., "Autobiography of a New 'Creatur': Female Spirituality, Selfhood, and Authorship in *The Book of Margery Kempe*", in Stanton D. (ed.), *The Female Autograph* (Chicago: The University of Chicago Press, 1984), pp. 57-68.

Myers M. D., "A Fictional-True Self: Margery Kempe and the Social Reality of the Merchant Elite of King's Lynn", *Albion. A Quarterly Journal Concerned with British Studies,* 31, 3 (1999), pp. 377-394.

Neuburger V., *Margery Kempe. A Study in Early English Feminism* (Berne, Berlin, New York: Peter Lang, 1994).

Parsons K., "The Red Ink Annotator of *The Book of Margery Kempe* and his Lay Audience", in Kerby-Fulton K. and M. Hilmo (eds), *The Medieval Professional Reader at Work: Evidence from Manuscripts of Chaucer, Langland, Kempe and Gower* (Victoria: ELS University of Victoria, 2001), pp. 143-158.

Partner N. F., "Studying Medieval Women. Sex, Gender, Feminism", *Speculum* 68, 2 (1993), pp. 305-308.

Ross R.C., "Oral Life, Written Text: The Genesis of *The Book of Margery Kempe*", *The Yearbook of English Studies,* 22 (1992), pp. 226-237.

Salih S., "Like A Virgin? *The Book of Margery Kempe*", in *Versions of Virginity in Late Medieval England* (Cambridge: D. S. Brewer, 2001), pp. 166-241.

Shklar R., "Cobham's Daughter: *The Book of Margery Kempe* and the Power of Heterodox Thinking", *The Modern Language Quarterly. A Journal of Literary History,* 56, 3 (1995), pp. 277-304.

Smith S., "The Book of Margery Kempe: This Creature's Unsealed Life", in *A Poetics of Women's Autobiography* (Bloomington: Indiana University Press, 1987), pp. 64-82.

Smith S. and J. Watson, *Reading Autobiography. A Guide for Interpreting Life Narratives* (second edition, Minneapolis: University of Minnesota Press, 2010).

Staley Johnson L., "The Trope of the Scribe and the Question of Literary Authority in the Works of Julian of Norwich and Margery Kempe", *Speculum* LXVI (1991), pp. 820-838.

Staley Johnson L., *Margery Kempe's Dissenting Fictions* (University Park, Pennsylvania: The Pennsylvania State University Press, 1994).

Stanton D.C. (ed.), *The Female Autograph* (Chicago & London: The University of Chicago Press, 1984).

Stewart A. (ed.), *The Book of the Wanderings of Brother Felix Fabri* (Palestine Pilgrim's Text Society, London, 1892-1893).

Tarvers J. K., "The Alleged Illiteracy of Margery Kempe: A Reconsideration of the Evidence", *Medieval Perspectives*, 11 (1996), pp. 113-124.

Thurston H., "Margery the Astonishing", *The Month* 168 (1936), pp. 446-456.

Walker Bynum C., "The Female Body and Religious Practice in the Later Middle Ages", in *Fragmentation and Redemption. Essays on Gender and the Human Body in Medieval Religion* (New York: Zone Books, 1991), pp. 181-238.

Watkin E. I., "In Defence of Margery Kempe", in *Poets and Mystics* (London: Sheed and Ward, 1953), pp. 104-134.

Webb D., "Women Pilgrims of the Middle Ages", *History Today*, 48, 7 (1998), pp. 20-26.

Windeatt B., (ed.), *The Book of Margery Kempe* (Harmondsworth: Penguin, 1985).

Windeatt B., "Introductory Essay" to *English Mystics of the Middle Ages* (Cambridge: Cambridge University Press, 1994), pp. 1-13.

Windeatt B., "Introduction: Reading and Re-reading *The Book of Margery Kempe*", in J. H. Arnold and K. J. Lewis (eds), *A

Companion to The Book of Margery Kempe (Cambridge: D. S. Brewer, 2004), pp. 1-16.

Wood Tuma G., *The Fourteenth Century English Mystics: A Comparative Analysis* (Salzburg: Universitat Salzburg, 1977).

Yoshikawa N. K., "Searching for the Image of New Ecclesia: Margery Kempe's Spiritual Pilgrimage Reconsidered", *Medieval Perspectives*, 11 (1996), pp. 125-138.

Yoshikawa N. K., "The Jerusalem Pilgrimage: The Centre of the Structure of the *Book of Margery Kempe*", *English Studies. A Journal of English Language and Literature*, 86, 3 (2005), pp. 193-205.

Further Reading

Arnold J. H. and K. J. Lewis (eds), *A Companion to* The Book of Margery Kempe (Cambridge: D. S. Brewer, 2004).

Atkinson C., *Mystic and Pilgrim: The Book and the World of Margery Kempe* (Ithaca, N.Y.: Cornell University Press, 1983).

Bowers T. N., "Margery Kempe as Traveler", *Studies in Philology*, 97, 1 (2000), pp. 1-28.

Campbell M. S., "'All My Children, Spiritual and Bodily': Love Transformed in *The Book of Margery Kempe*", *The Journal of the Association for the Interdisciplinary Study of the Arts*, 1 (1995), pp. 59-69.

Colledge E., *The Mediaeval Mystics of England* (London: John Murray, 1962).

Dickman S., "A Showing of God's Grace: *The Book of Margery Kempe*", in Pollard W. F. and R. Boenig (eds), *Mysticism and Spirituality in Medieval England* (Cambridge: D. S. Brewer, 1997), pp. 159-176.

Dillon J., "The Making of Desire in *The Book of Margery Kempe*", *Leeds Studies in English*, XXVI (1995), pp. 113-144.

Fienberg N., "Thematics of Value in *The Book of Margery Kempe*", *Modern Philology*, 87, 2 (1989), pp. 132-141.

Helfers J. P., "The Mystic as Pilgrim: Margery Kempe and the Tradition of Nonfictional Travel Narrative", *Rocky Mountain Medieval and Renaissance Association*, 13 (1992), pp. 25-45.

Hirsch J. C., "Author and Scribe in *The Book of Margery Kempe*", *Medium Aevum*, XLIV (1975), pp. 145-150.

Holbrook S. E., "'About Her' Margery Kempe's Book of Feeling and Working", in Dean J. M. and C. K. Zacher (eds), *The Idea of Medieval Literature: New Essays on Chaucer and Medieval Culture in Honor of Donald R. Howard* (Newark: University of Delaware Press, 1992), pp. 265-284.

Howes L., "On the Birth of Margery Kempe's Last Child", *Modern Philology: A Journal Devoted to Research in Medieval and Modern Literature*, 90, 2, (1992), pp. 220-225.

Kelliher H., "The Rediscovery of Margery Kempe: A Footnote", *The British Library Journal*, 22 (1996), pp. 259-263.

Lochrie K., *Margery Kempe and Translations of the Flesh* (Philadelphia: University of Pennsylvania Press, 1991).

Magners L., "Annotated Bibliography on Margery Kempe", <http://web.archive.org/web/20080219123238re_/chass.colostate-pueblo.edu/history/seminar/kempe/kempebib.htm>, last accessed November 2010.

Margherita G., "Margery Kempe and the Pathology of Writing", in *The Romance of Origins. Language and Sexual Difference in Middle English Literature* (Philadelphia: University of Pennsylvania Press, 1994), pp. 15-42.

McEntire S. J. (ed.), *Margery Kempe: A Book of Essays* (New York: Garland Publishing, 1992).

Mullini R., "Voci di donne nel Medio Evo inglese", *Merope,* XI, 27 (1999), pp. 5-41.

Slade C., "Alterity in Union: The Mystical Experience of Angela of Foligno and Margery Kempe", *Religion and Literature*, 23, 3 (1991), pp. 109-126.

Staley Johnson L., "Margery Kempe: Social Critic", *The Journal of Medieval and Renaissance Studies,* 22 (1992), pp. 159-184.

Stargardt U., "The Beguines of Belgium, the Dominican Nuns of Germany, and Margery Kempe", in Heffernan T. J. (ed.), *The Popular Literature of Medieval England* (Knoxville: The University of Tennessee Press, 1985), pp. 277-313.

Stone R. K., *Middle English Prose Style. Margery Kempe and Julian of Norwich* (The Hague/Paris: Mouton, 1970).

Uhlman D. R., "The Comfort of Voice, the Solace of Script: Orality and Literacy in *The Book of Margery Kempe*", *Studies in Philology,* 91 (1994), pp. 50-69.

Wilson J., "Communities of Dissent: The Secular and Ecclesiastical Communities of Margery Kempe's Book", in Watt D. (ed.), *Medieval Women and Their Communities* (Toronto: University of Toronto Press, 1997), pp. 155-185.

Wright M. J., "What They Said to Margery Kempe: Narrative Reliability in her Book", *Neophilologus,* LXXIX, 1 (1995), pp. 497-508.